THE TRUTH IS
IN THE NUMBERS

THE TRUTH IS
IN THE NUMBERS

Doug Allen

To order additional copies of this book, contact:
Xlibris Corporation
1-888-795-4274
www.Xlibris.com
Orders@Xlibris.com
41491

CONTENTS

Introduction 9

Chapter 1:   Wealth Building 1A 11
Chapter 2:   Investor Attitude 19
Chapter 3:   Financing 30
Chapter 4:   Approaching An Investment............................. 38
Chapter 5:   Due Diligence 48
Chapter 6:   Endless Opportunity 56
Chapter 7:   Five Star Tenants 66
Chapter 8:   Shifting markets 75
Chapter 9:   Foreclosures 82
Chapter 10:   Note Investing 89
Chapter 11:   New Construction 98
Chapter 12:   A Balanced Portfolio 103
Chapter 13:   Asset Protection 109
Chapter 14:   My Story...115

Conclusion 121
About The Author... 123

Dedications

I would like to dedicate this book to my late father, Donald Richard Allen. It was my dad who told me since a young age that it was important for me to buy a house. Little did he know that I would take it to such an extreme. He was always a supporter of mine and I loved him dearly. He was one of few I could talk of my success in real estate with and bounce ideas off without him feeling jealous or as if I was bragging. Individuals like that are rare, and he was a rare individual.

Introduction

How many times have I been to a free workshop or conference or seminar with the promise of finding out all the secrets of how to make money in real estate? Well I can tell you, more times than I'd like to admit. Only to be teased with just a taste of information. How many times have I sat through the whole thing and found out at the end that I'll need to buy some expensive package, or go to some expensive workshop, so that I can get the information that I so desperately want? Too many times. I've even been to these meetings when I was a 20 year real estate investor, hopeful to hear some new idea or some new slant on an existing idea that would change my way of thinking or get me motivated. The more I go these days, the less motivated I've become to continue going. Why cant they just give you the information you want and be done with it? Because it's all about getting their hooks in you and your money. I've decided to finally give you all my up front and personal look of real estate investing. In this book you'll find a realistic view into the art of wealth building and real estate investing. Simple formulas and a hard look at varibles that can affect your bottom line. I have found that investing in real estate is not a get rich quick scheme, however profitable, it's a road to financial freedom that if maneuvered correctly can bring a lifetime of satisfaction in half the time. The title, The Truth Is In The Numbers, refers to the simplistic approach I personally have taken to become a multimillionaire in the real estate game. There are many factors to acquiring wealth. We will discuss those factors that I feel are of the essences to become wealthy. I will share with you my personal experiences and explain the way I break those experiences down, so you can understand the reasoning behind doing something, good or bad. My goal in this book is to get you familiar and comfortable with the thought of real estate investing and familiar with words used in the investing game. Comfortable with knowing how to confidently apply what you've learned in this book, to an investing approach and a life approach. Being able to make money in real estate and know you're doing the right thing will all come together as you take one investment at a time. In the course of examining each one of those investments you will know that it is a safe investment or not because the truth is in the numbers.

Chapter 1

Wealth Building 1A

In this first chapter I think it's important to go over some basic rules of wealth building. You have to put a concrete foundation in before you start building a house. So you must have some basic principles on building wealth before you're actually able to build it.

No matter what level you're on, you have to maintain that level to be able to get to the next one. What I mean by that is live below your means. No matter how much money you make, always make sure you have some of that money set aside after all the bills are paid. That means, in the beginning, when you're just getting started, make sure you open a savings account, with no ATM card. Pay yourself first, in the form of putting some of that money you've worked so hard to make, right in that savings account. Be excited about it. Watch your wealth begin to grow right away. Don't touch it, let it grow and grow. It's much easier to save money when you can't touch it. Your pocket is not a place for savings. Pocket money seems to fly right out just about as quick as it goes in. So please get a savings account right away. Soon that money will be able to do something for you, but for now that savings account is your net worth.

Don't go out and get something with payments, unless that thing is a house that you can afford. Now, in the beginning is not the time to be buying anything that does not appreciate(go up in value). If you have a job, and let's say that job pays $1500 take home per month, don't set yourself up to be spending $1500 a month. Set yourself up to be spending $1000 per month and put

$500 a month away in that new savings account of yours. Be super conservative with all your money and remember that you're now on your way towards wealth building. A penny saved is a penny earned. It's really important in the beginning. The reason is that money makes money and you have to have money to make money. There will be plenty of time to enjoy your money when there is enough to enjoy.

Let your money work for itself. Make it pull its own weight, just as you do. Even if that means just finding the best home for it. A free savings account is a good start. One that pays a good interest rate is even better. If you're not planning on touching that money for a while, try putting some or all of that money in a certificate of deposit if you can get an even better interest rate of return on it. Interest is an amazing thing, make it work for you.

Establish some credit if you don't already have it. If you have none right now, start applying for some credit cards. At first, try for a small line with your local clothing store or gas station. Then move up the ladder quickly. You'll be suprised how many people want to offer you cards after you have your first one. The key here is to have that credit and not use it. You can use it lightly like charging an item or two, but have the money to be able to pay it off immediately. You're merely trying to build a credit history, not make someone else rich on the interest they're charging you. Your goal is to get the biggest line of credit as possible on a visa. So if you don't have 10, 15 or $20,000 or more, keep reapplying to increase your available limit.

These lines of credit will do three things for you. First, they will show to the world that you are trustworthy enough to have credit and not do something crazy with it, like charge all your cards to the limit on some worthless personal property. Second, they might just make you some money. I once had a visa with a $30,000 limit. It just so happened they sent me an offer for me to borrow that money interest free for 6 months. I turned around and loaned that money out, secured to a piece of real estate, for 12% annually. That would be an $1800 dollar profit over 6 months on someone elses money. But it gets better, I was a liscensed real estate agent at the time so I actually shared in a portion of the fee that the broker charged to make that loan. There will be other opportunities to make money using other peoples money(opm) this was just one instance for me. You first have to have the credit available to you before you are able to use it, so make sure you keep your new found credit in good standing. The third thing your credit might do for you is help you out in a pinch. The need for short term cash in some instances is inevitable. There is any number of reasons why you might need some cash for a short term period. You don't want to get caught in a cycle where you're borrowing money from your credit every month to pay bills. However, it's possible to be in a situation where you have a need for some short term money. Your tax return might be coming in next week but your rent is due today. You don't want to be evicted, so you need some short term cash. Be careful how and when you use this money from your credit cards. Not only is it a bad habit to get into but you will pay the price as well. Not all, but many of these credit cards charge what they call a cash advance fee. Seek ways to avoid these fees when you are in such a pinch. I was in need of short term cash on more than one occasion. One such occasion was when I had bought a house in the hopes of fixing it up and selling it for a profit. The fix it and holding costs were more than I had expected and I soon ran out of money. I had to finish the house so I could sell it and recoup my cash investment, and hopefully some profit. In this instance I used my credit cards to purchase the items I needed to finish the house. Fortunately, with the use of this short term cash, I was able to finish the house, sell it, and walk away with a $30,000 profit. Of course I immediately paid back my credit cards and put a healthy sum in my savings account with no ATM card.

Your net worth is your assets minus your liabilities. I am constantly determining my net worth because it fluxuates all the time. You too should keep a close eye on your net worth. It is like

13

a physical on your financial health. If you have $2000 in the bank, a car worth $5000 that you owe $3000 on, and personal property like furniture, jewelry, clothes, etc. worth $2000, your net worth is $6000. You'd better get busy out in the world and start to increase that amount. At least it's not in the negative. Your mission, should you decide to accept it, is to increase your net worth. Many people are never even aware what net worth is so you're already 1 step ahead of a lot of people. Don't falsely inflate your net worth to yourself by thinking your stuff is worth more than you know it to be. I always figure a value of something by asking myself this question. How much cold hard cash can I get for that item right now? That's the value I place on it and the amount I figure in for my net worth at that time. Your net worth can go up and down in a given month depending on the time of month you calculate it. Be aware of that fact and know your limits of financial strength.

You have to be a good manager of money as you're on this road of wealth building. Budgeting is a good idea but there certainly needs to be some flexability within that budget. There will always be some unexpected cost come up as you go through life. There were many times when I felt like I was getting ahead financially and then got slapped back into reality by something like my tires being bald and needing new ones. Tires are expensive and can set you back considerably. In being a good manager of money you have to look for ways, constantly, to save it. I have many times looked at alternative methods instead of going out and spending a lot of money on something. Many times that alternative has been curbing my appetite for that thing I desired. In the case of tires, I coudn't drive on completely bald ones, and they were very bald. However, I found a different avenue. Instead of going out and purchasing new tires, at the cost of $125 per tire, I went out and bought some used ones at $30 per tire. They don't advertise these tires. You have to ask and follow the tire guy into the back of the store to see if they even have your size. You might have to go to more than one tire store. I didn't want to spend the money, so I spent what I did have and that was the time to go look for a deal. It paid off in the form of $380 savings for 4 tires. That's being a good money manager. I saved money because I was willing to spend some time. Look before you leap. There's ways to save money on everything. In saving money, you're increasing your net worth because there's more to count in your account.

Writing down your goals about anything is a very effective way of attaining those goals. Financial goals are no different. It's important to put on paper where you want to be at any given time. If you keep it in your head and don't write it down, it tends to slip away as your mind concentrates on the task at hand. I would recommend writing down your 1 year goals. If you want to have a certain amount of money in the bank in 1 year, say $12,000, write it down. You can then write down your 6 month goals which of course would be $6,000. Break it down further to monthly goals of $1,000 per month. Finally down to weekly goals of $250. By taking a yearly goal and breaking it down to weekly goals you can check yourself along the way to make sure you're on track. If you're saving $250 per week with no problem, you know your yearly goal is on track to be met. Adjustmets can be made at any given time to your overall plan. Have some flexability so you can succeed. You'll feel a real sense of accomplishment as you start to realize your goals. This will build in you a serious feeling of being able to achieve what you set out to do and you'll have the simple math to check the equation. This way of setting longer term goals by writing them down and then breaking them down into shorter term goals that align with the longer term ones so you can know you're on track or make some adjustments is a must to achieving those goals.

Visualization is also an effective way to get what you're after. If you can visualize it, you can have it or do it. You can use this method for anything. All you have to do is put yourself into the situation, visually, that you're wanting. Whether it be some athletic skill or some object you desire it helps to actually see yourself in your mind attaining that skill or object. There are whole books designed specificly to address this method of acquiring what you want. It can be a very effective tool.

Nothing replaces hard work. If you're a hard worker people will notice you. No matter what you're doing, be the best you can be at that task. This will get you very far in life and wealth. If you're working for someone else for an hourly wage, extra hours are a good thing, that's more money you can sock away for yourself and your net worth. The more money you save in the beginning, the easier it is for you later on. The sooner your money can start working for you instead of you working for your money the better. If you're working for yourself, you know how important it is to be, not only a hard worker, but also how to work smart. Working smart and hard work goes hand in hand. Don't waste time, it's a valued commodity. Don't put off until tommorrow what you can do today. It's an old saying that still rings true today. Don't let tasks overwhelm you. Do as much as you can in a given day and start again the next day.

Knowledge about anything you're doing is essential. The more knowledge you have about something, the easier you'll be able to conquer it. Knowledge is power and the opposite of fear. Knowing the ins and outs and shortcuts of a given subject allows you to navigate that road smoothly and effectively. Acquiring the knowledge you need on anything will take some determination on your part. If you seek it you will find it. Knowledge is everywhere. It comes to you in many forms. There's book knowledge, there's personal experience, there's training and even friends that can give you the knowledge you're after. Education is very valuable and something that can never be taken away from you. You can give a poor person a million dollars and they'll be poor again in a short amount of time, but you can take a millionaires money away and they will be a millionaire again because they have the knowledge about how to become a millionaire. This is the power of knowledge.

Determination can go a long way as well. If you're determined to do something there's nothing or no one person that will stand in the way of your success. Shrug off all the nay sayers and don't let them step on your dreams. If there's something in your mind that you want to accomplish then go for it. If at first you don't succeed, then try, try again. When I was buying, fixing up and selling properties I felt pretty good about what I was doing. Then came a drop in the real estate market and I couldn't expect to sell those same properties as quick as I had in the past, there just wasn't as huge of a demand for them as there had been. That, coupled with the fact that the price had dropped considerably on them, made it not such a good atmosphere for buying, fixing and selling. So I moved to a new, different way of making money in real estate. I'll get into it more in the book later, but basicly I started to buy properties to hold them for the extra money that was available from the rent after the principle, interest, taxes, insurance and utilities (pitiu) had been paid. Many of the people I told about what I was doing said I was crazy and that I was doing the wrong thing, but to me the truth was in the numbers and I didn't listen to them. It's a good thing I didn't to, because if I had listened to them I would have never compiled the amount of properties I did and would have never experienced the wealth that I now enjoy. I was determined and I wasn't going to let anyone stand in my way. I'm a big believer in math and numbers and formulas. To me it's something you can rely on. It's as simple as knowing that 5+3=8 and being able to double check that by 8-3=5. I'm a numbers guy because you can count on numbers steadiness, reliability and checkability. Tride and true formulas have been able to explain everything in this world and I believe they can explain the simple viability of an investment for you.

When you're first getting started on the road of wealth building and financial independence you must have some money coming in (cash flow). Whether your cash flow is a job or a business or an inheritance or any other number of income streams, it makes no difference, as long as you have income. If you have no income you have nothing to save. You have no money to be good with. So go get a job. No, this is not financial independence, you're just getting started. You have to crawl before you walk. You have just started on the road of wealth building. You're on level 1, and remember you have to maintain that level before you can go to the next. You're laying your concrete foundation so that soon you can start building your house. Maintain this level for 1 year. Keep your income stream or job by not being late and by being a hard, determined worker. Establish some credit and don't get crazy with it by charging your credit up to max balance. Start a savings plan by writing your financial goals down and sticking with that plan. Live below your means by way of budgeting and not purchasing any big ticket items that will stretch your financial strength. Think of your financial strength as a muscle that you're trying to build up. You have to lift 20, 30 and 50 pounds many times as you work your way up to lifting 200 pounds. You don't just step up and lift 200 pounds right away without the expectation of pulling a muscle or hurting yourself permanently. You have to work your way up until you're comfortable lifting that amout of weight. Same is true with financial strength. You don't go out and purchase a $20,000 car with a payment of $350, just because it's fabulous, when all your income monthly is $1500 and the rest of your bills total $1000. That's stretching your financial strength. That's like trying to lift 200 pounds your first day of lifting. Where's your savings figure into this scenario. Try buying a car for $1,000. It might not be as fabulous but it wont break you financially for a long time to come. There'll be plenty of time to buy your dream car once you get your financial house in order. For now just concentrate on maintaining level 1 and not driving off the wealth building road.

Chapter 2

Investor Attitude

So you've been maintaining your income stream for a while now and you've managed to save some money and you feel like you're ready to graduate to level 2 because level 1 has become quite boring for you. You've established some credit lines and haven't maxed them out. You're living well below your means and some of your goals have been met or are well on their way to being met. Good job, you're well on your way to the top. Let's now start focusing on some streams of cash flow that will endure whether you're there or not. Let's also start becoming familiar with some of the terminology used in real estate circles. Let's start developing the investor attitude.

For me real estate is the only investment. I've tried other avenues and have never recieved the success as I have had with real estate. Real estate is defined as real property. All other things are personal property and most personal property does not go up in value as does real property. This way in which an item goes up in value is know as appreciation. Anything that goes up in value or appreciates will have some equity in them. Real estate is not the only thing that will appreciate, but it's one of few. As an asset appreciates your net worth will go up. Your net worth will only go up if your name is on the title of that asset. Equity is the difference between what you paid for that asset and what that asset can now be sold for. This figures into your net worth in the sense that if you did sell that asset you would have that cash influx at that time. This simple knowledge about appreciating real estate has built the fortunes for many in this nation. Certainly the key to becoming wealthy in real estate is through long term ownership of real property, real estate. Knowing how to hold this real property effectively for the long term is really just a simple numbers game.

The most important investment you'll ever make is the purchase of a house for yourself. As you own that house it will appreciate and therefore you will have some inherent equity in that home. In many cases I've seen the appreciation of a home go up so fast it has out paced any other income stream that person might have. Talk about being on the fast track to building net worth and financial freedom, that's big. Just by owning a home that you're using to live in, your net worth is increasing dramaticly. Of course you have to have a big enough income stream to be able to afford that house in the first place. You'll probably have to get qualified for a loan to buy that house unless you've been really good with saving your money and you're going to pay cash for that house. Even then I don't know that I would recommend paying cash. If indeed you are getting a loan to buy that house, keep in mind the simple rules in chapter one. Don't stretch your financial strength and make sure you still have savings set up in your budget. You don't want that house to break you financially by having the payment so high that you're stretching to make the payment every month. When buying a home for yourself you want to make sure of two things, you're going to be comfortable in that house and that it's something that you can afford comfortably. Don't make the mistake of trying to buy your dream house right away. Get something that's modest and fits your financial picture. Just because you're qualified for a $300,000 loan, that doesn't mean you have to go out and buy one for that price. I see too many people trying buy for $305,000 when they're qualified for a $300,000 loan. Look for one that is priced between $200,000 and $250,000. You wont be in this house forever and there will be plenty of time down the road to get that dream house of yours.

If you do indeed buy a house to live in and that house appreciates substantially in a short amount of time, well beyond your present income stream, don't be overwhelmed. You've been very lucky and now you have to handle your new found wealth in a responsible manner. This house will not continue to appreciate like this always. Still keep within your income stream and continue to budget and have that savings as always. Don't think because now that your house has gone up in value so much that you can throw everything else out the window, start charging your cards up, forget saving money, and live like royalty. This is only the beginning, and a great start, of what could be your ticket to financial freedom and lots of wealth. Don't mess it up by treating that house of yours as a bank account that has only withdrawl slips. I've seen too many people who have had a house appreciate and they have become overwhelmed with their new found, what they think, is wealth. They'll work themselves into a bad financial way and then bail themselves out by borrowing on that house to make things right. Then they do it again and again because they know they have the equity in the house to bail them out. This is a very bad practice because you're throwing away a chance at becoming very rich. Don't borrow your new found eqiuty in that home unless the money you're borrowing is going to make you more money and increase your overall net worth. That equity in your home is your future not your wallet.

I believe in the bottom of the market scenario. In the bottom of the market is where you'll find the most buyers who can qualify to buy a home. Entry level housing is where most of the activity is at any given time. In a down market and in a good market the majority of purchases take place in the lowest price range there is. A basic rule in economics is if the demand for something is high and the availability for something is low, then the price will go up. If the demand is low and the availability high then the price will go down. This is the law of supply and demand. In the low end of the real estate market you have a better ratio of appreciation than you do on higher end homes. Many people refer to the median price of a home. This is a price in which half of the houses in a given area sell above and half of the houses sell below. Work below that median price when looking for a house for yourself, for now. Work below that median price when looking for an investment property always. There are many reason to stay below the median price when looking for an investment property, whether you're looking to buy a fixer to flip or buy something to hold for a period of time. One of those reasons is holding costs. You want to pay out as little as possible in principle, interest, taxes, insurance and utilities (pitiu) during the time you are rehabing this property for resale if it's a fixer to flip. When you're done with the rehab you want to be in a price range where you'll have the most buyers looking at your finished product, that way it sells quicker. The worst thing is having a vacant house on your hands. You're making the payment, not recieving any rent and it's vulnerable to vandalisim. If it's a holder the same is true. You want your costs of holding to be as little as they can be so you can maximize the rent you recieve.

While holding down your steady stream of income, start to become familiar with what houses are selling for in the area you live. We call this market familiarity. You want to become in touch with what prices are in your area so you can spot a buy when you see it. If you know that all the houses in a given area are selling for right around $200,000 and you find one that is selling for $100,000 you might just have a good deal on your hands. You would never know it was a deal though if you didn't have some level of market familiarity. The house might also need $100,000 in fixing and it's no deal at all, you never know until you do some investigation into that specific property. This investigation is referred to as due diligence. Another reason for getting it touch with prices in your neighborhood is to see if it makes sense to start buying some of these properties for holders or long term investments. When spotting a buy you have to move quickly because buys wont be on the market for long. Many other people are looking for a deal on real property as well. Start having the investor attitude and be ready to buy something that makes sense. You can do this by making an informed decision and checking the numbers. If that $100,000 house in a $200,000 neighborhood is in need of $25,000 worth of work and can be done being fixed in a couple of months of after work and weekend hours, then maybe it is a good buy. Figure in the holding costs, closing costs, real estate commission costs and any other costs that may be associated with the transaction and you'll have a good idea of what you're going to make after the sale. Figure the price you're going to sell for to be the best price in the neighborhood. After all, you want to sell this property quick and not be sitting on a vacant hosuse for any period of time. Give someone a deal on that house so you can make a quick buck and move on to the next one.

Start associating yourself with people involved in real estate. Whether it be realtors, lenders, other investors, title companies, or some type of investor club. All these types of people will be as excited as you to talk about real estate. Hear some success stories and how they did whatever it is they did to make a buck in real estate. Hear some of their failures so you know what to avoid. Being a real estate investor is really a state of mind and a fancy title for someone who profits in some way from real estate transactions. You can be that person. Get some business cards that say so. There is a wide range of investors, from the person who is buying his or hers very first fixer or holder to a person like Donald Trump who has more properties than he can even count. You are all real estate investors. Having that attitude will help you immensely in establishing who you are. You're an entrepreneur in every way.

When meeting realtors ask them if there are any great buys that they know about and how they think the overall market is at this time, prepare to get an earfull. If they say yes that they do have a great buy on a piece of real estate somewhere in the area, ask them why it's such a great buy. Realtors work on commission so it might just be a good buy because he or she is the one the seller has hired to sell that piece of property. Then again he or she might want you as a client and this piece of property he or she is telling you about does have some real potential for you to make some extra money on in some way. You make that decision after you've checked it out. Get their card, ask them if they can show you the property as soon as possible (A.S.A.P.). In every instance have the buyer beware attitude. Even if you think this property is a steal for what they're asking, don't show it, you're just beginning the negotiation process and you don't want anyone to know how you feel about the deal you're getting ready to get. Who knows, you might be able to get an even better deal on this piece if you just play your cards right. Your realtor should have all the contracts so that you can make an offer on the property. If there are a few people interested in the property you're looking at, make a reasonable offer right away and hopefully you can get it accepted. In all real estate contracts there is time provided for you to do some due diligence and still be able to not buy the house, usually about 10-14 days. Once you have an accepted offer is when you really have to spend serious time getting to know the ins and outs of this property to see if it's really a good deal. At least you've got rid of the competition by making your offer first and now you know your due diligence will not be wasted. Always get a termite report and preferably have the seller pay for that report. This will not only point out any bug infestation the property might have but will also point out any dry rot or water damage that will need to be fixed, probably by you.

When talking to any lenders ask them what kind of great financing they might have and what's the best deal with the least money for a down payment. 100% financing is always great but it might be a little more expensive than if you put down 5% of the purchase price. Working with other peoples money (opm) is always a good way to go because it allows you to have less risk in a given project. There's always money out there in one form or another to be able to do what you want in real estate. It's the deal that dictates the availability of those funds. If you have a super deal on a property every lender in town will want to loan you the money to buy it. The reason is because they know their money is safe if you're getting a great buy on the property. Don't isolate yourself with only one lender. Have many of them that you can call or get a loan through. There are many different types of lenders as well. There are brokers who have many different lenders they can give your loan to. There are direct lenders who generally have the most reasonable costs to borrow money but have tougher standards on the house and the borrower. There's also hard money lenders who really don't care much about the borrowers but care about the house and if there's enough equity in the property to lend on. Whichever lender you're working with, ask them to nail down the fees they're going to charge you to borrow the money by asking them to give you a good faith estimate (GFE). This (GFE) will also give you the interest rate they're charging you and the total payment on that loan. This is all important information when getting a loan.

Other investors are great people to talk to when you're wanting to become an investor yourself. Being a real estete investor is tough in the sense that there are no guidelines or rules to follow and many times, as you're acting as an investor, it feels as if you're trying to walk a straight line, although that line is invisable. That's why it is important to talk to other investors. Investors who specialize in the area in which you're going to focus your energy on. Some real estate investors are buying properties to fix up then sell, only. Some are buying for the positve cash flow (rent - pitiu = pcf). These investors do have other options such as refinancing to increase their operating income. Some are buying vacant lots so they can build a new house on it and sell that for a profit. Some are buying bigger parcels of land to split down and sell those smaller portions for a profit. Some are working forclosures. Some are purchasing existing 1st and 2nd deeds of trusts at a discount. Some are lending money to other investors for projects and sharing in the profits after the deal is closed. As you can see there are many areas of expertise within this real estate investor heading. These are some of the legitimate ways investors make money in the real estate field. Some are doing a combination of these things as to increase their income. I've also heard of many different variations and ploys to get novice investors into the game so that others could profit. Be careful, it's a jungle out there. There is risk in real estate investing no doubt, that's why there is so much profit available in it. You can however, minimize that risk by doing your homework and staying clear of what might not be such a viable investment. Other investors can help you with directing you toward your homework and by helping you assess the viability of any investment. Maybe you can take on a mentor in the investing game. Investors who have been in the game for a while love the excitement of a new investor. Especially if they've been in the game for a while because they know what it takes to continue to be in business.

Title companies are great allies to have as a real estate investor. Don't ever buy a piece of real property without having a title policy issued on it at the time of purchase. This is much like an insurance policy that guarentees that there are no additional liens on the property you're buying. This and your relationship with a title company is very important. Title companies can do much more for you than just handle your transaction. This transaction period, the time between which you have an accepted offer and when you actually own the property is called the escrow period. By opening up an escrow with your preferred title company, you've initiated the beginning of a given transaction process whether it be the buying or selling of a real property. The title company will act as a neutral 3rd party to that transaction to help facilitate the close of that deal. If you are purchasing a property that you plan to sell again within the next year or two, ask your specific title company about purchasing a binder for the property. By purchasing a binder on a property that you plan to sell soon, you can save yourself some money on title fees when you go to sell it. The title company can also supply you information on properties that might be a potential project for you. I have bought many properties by seeing a beat, fixer in an acceptable neighborhood and then taking that address to the title company and asking them to supply me with the owners name, address and even possibly their phone number. I have then called or written them and expressed my intention of buying that house. When contacting them in this manner, don't tell them that you're planning on fixing the house up and selling it for a huge profit. Merely tell them that you've been looking for a house in the neighborhood and are interested in theirs. What you're going to do with it after you own it is irrelevant. The important thing is that you both come to a reasonable sale price that's a winner for both of you, so ask them how much they will sell it for. No matter what price they give you tell them that you'll write up an offer and how can you get it to them. If they wont give you a price and continue to insist that you tell them what you'll give them for it, then simply say you'll figure it out and send them an offer by fax or through the mail. Usually the first person to say the price will get the worst of the deal so push them to say what they'll take for it. If they wont then start low on your offering scale. If they do say a price and it's well below what you thought you might get it for, save your jubilation until after you're off the phone. If they do not accept your offer, then leave the conversation in a respectable manner. Tell them thank you very much and if they change their mind to please give you a call. You will be surprised how many of them will call you back and be ready to deal at a later date. The title company will only expect you to run this transaction through their office once you have a deal and that is the least you can do for them after they've given you the key to the golden lock so to speak. Every title company has a sales representive that you can speak with and they will gladly tell you how they can help you identify, verify and solidify any real estate transaction.

If there is a real estate investor club in your area, try to go to a meeting or two. There are a few different types of investor meetings. Some of them want each member to put into a pool of money so that the group can do some investing with that money, with you now being a part of that group. Others get together and merely discuss trends of the market in your area and different methods of investing. They might even get as specific as to discuss certain market niches or areas of investment or even certain properties to invest in. Either way you go or whatever group you decide to go to, the exposure is good. Anytime you can get involved in a real estate discussion with other people concerning investments you can usually come away with something good. Experience is certainly of value when talking to anyone on the subject. If there is no investor meeting in your area maybe you can start one and bring in people with knowledge on the subject as a guest speaker. It can be a relatively short meeting with any kind of format you wish. The main thing is getting in and talking real estate. Not everyone will have the fever for investing. Some are not comfortable with the risk and others are just happy to be part of the 9 to 5 club. Some will never own a house of their own because their parents rented houses their whole lives and that's all they're comfortable with doing. That's alright though, we all need long term tenants to pay off our mortgaged properties so more power to them. When we do find someone who is excited to talk about investing and getting ahead financially, we love it. We feed on each other and bounce ideas back and forth until we find some idea that seems to be the best or the best way to make money in real estate.

Obtaining a real estate agents liscense is something you may want to consider putting on your to do list. It's not a hard thing to do. There are many companies out there who would be glad to help you for a nominal fee. You take a couple of courses called principles and then you're ready to take the test. Right before you take the test you can get an overview so you can pass it the first time. If you fail the test you are able to take it again in a short time after the first. By having your liscense you can have access to the metrolist service for your area. The metrolist service is a posting site where all real estate agents can post what they have for sale. There are also many training courses held at your local realtor board. These courses can be very helpful for an investor because all of them pertain to things surrounding the real estate field. Others pertain directly to the investor. Networking possibilities are another great feature of having your liscense. Once you have your liscense you'll have to hang it with a broker and arrange a commission split. In that brokerage house you'll find others with similar views and stratagies toward investing. You don't have to do this on a full time basis, you can do it part time, as many do. This liscense will allow you to pocket a commission on a property you are buying, if it's listed, and therefore reducing your overall cost for that property. If you choose to get your liscense you can also take a listing. Taking a listing is merely signing a contract with a seller on a piece of property in which they hire you to market that property for a commission. Usually that commission is about 3% for the listing agent and 3% to the selling agent. If you list it and sell it, you get about 6%. That's called double ending the deal. You can also represent a buyer who is looking to buy either a house for themselves or an investment property. In this transaction you would be the buyers agent or the selling agent and when that deal closes escrow you'll be recieving a check for approximately 3% of the purchase price. Actually your broker would be recieving the check and then you would get your agreed upon split of that check. Either way obtaining a liscense can get you some extra money and get you in some circles of people involved in real estate.

Chapter 3

Financing

In real estate, financing is one of the keys to unlocking the door. The right loan for the right house is essential in determining whether you're going to make money on the deal. You must have a good idea about what you're going to do with the real estate and how long you're going to be keeping it when making a decision as to which loan you're going to get on that property. Although plans change, knowing what you're going to do with your real estate will help narrow down the financing options. You wouldn't want to get a loan that has a 2 year prepayment penalty, on a property that you're planning on selling in just a few months. There are many different lenders with many different loans out there in the world. When someone or some company makes you a loan on a specific piece of property, they're using that property as collateral for that loan. They secure that loan to that property with a document known as a deed of trust and that deed of trust gets recorded at the county recorders office in the county where the property is located. Along with your signature on the deed of trust you'll sign the actual note which has all the terms and conditions pertaining to that loan. The grant deed to the property, which is like the pink slip to a vehicle, goes in your name because you're holding title to that property. If you were paying cash for that property then only that grant deed would need to be recorded at the county recorders office. If you're buying that house for say $100,000 and there's a company who is loaning you all $100,000 then you are getting 100% financing and there would be a deed of trust recorded at the same time the grant deed was recorded. In this instance the $100,000 deed of trust would be considered a 1st deed of trust. If you're buying for $100,000 and you're borrowing $75,000 from one company and $25,000 from another, you're still getting 100% financing but you'll have 2 deeds of trusts recorded on the property. The $75,000 loan will be considered the 1st deed and the $25,000 will be considered the 2nd deed of trust. It doesn't matter which amount is larger, it matters which deed of trust is recorded first. If the $25,000 is recorded first then it becomes the 1st deed of trust. If they're being sent at the same time then there's instructions from the lender or title company as to who is in first and who is in second position. If you're getting 100% financing it means you're borrowing all the money it takes to purchase the property and the loan to value or (LTV) is 100%. If you're buying a property for $100,000 and you're putting 10% down or $10,000 and borrowing 90% or $90,000 then your LTV is 90%.

You want to get the best loan for a purchase or a refinance as you possibly can. Refinancing is getting a new loan on a property you already own. To get the best loan on anything there are a series of questions you need to ask your lender prior to getting that loan and double check those answers by looking for it in writing within the actual note when signing it. A GFE or good faith estimate should cover most of your questions but not all of them. You want to question what the total cost of getting that loan is? What the interest rate is on that loan? How long of a term the loan is for or when will the loan be paid off? What is the cost of the title fees involved in the transaction? Is the payment on the loan an interest only payment and therefore the loan will never be paid off until the whole amount becomes due and payable at some time in the future? If so then when is that date? Is there a prepayment penalty, be it soft or hard, on the loan so you can pay the loan off, either by refinancing or selling at anytime without being charged extra money? A soft prepayment penalty is one that you're only charged if you get a new loan or refinance the property and not charged if you actually sell the property. A hard prepayment penalty will be charged regardless if you're refinancing or selling. What is the payment on the loan based on the interest rate? These are all important questions to ask your lender. If the payment on the loan is $1,000 then that's the principle and interest or p&i portion of the pitiu formula. You then have to figure out how much the property taxes and the insurance is, that's the t&i portion of the pitiu formula. Then finally, if you are responsible to pay any portion of the utilities, that would be the u in pitiu. So your p&i is $1,000 monthly and let's say your t&i is $200 monthly and your u is $50 monthly. Your total pitiu is $1,250. That is your total financial commitment monthly to this property. Can you afford this amount?

Financing is usually the main reason why real estate deals fall through or don't close. In most cases it's because of an overzealous lender who wants to do the financing so they can make some money but then can never produce those funds needed to get the deal closed. They'll give you all kinds of reasons why the loan went south on you, some of them might even be true. When you find a lender who can produce, or get the deal closed in a timely fashion with the terms they promised in the beginning, then they should be high on your list of lenders to use on the next deal. If you're the one who is needing the financing then you should start to shop around immediately for the best loan. By doing this you will become a prequalified buyer. Sellers and sellers agents love to see a prequalified buyer who is making an offer on a property of theirs. It means that you have already been to a lender who has approved you for a loan to buy in a certain price range. The lender you are working with will gladly supply you with a letter stating so and you should attach that letter along with the offer when submitting it to the seller or sellers agent. When it's you who has picked the lender you have much more control over the deal. It's much easier to put your finger on the pulse of the deal so you know what's going on or what's not going on.

Appraisals are a must on almost every deal. Lenders will need to get an appraisal on the property they are going to loan on from a third party not involved in the transaction. Appraisers are good people to know if you're not that familiar with how to establish a value for a property. Some of them will actually give you a value of about how much they'll appraise it for before you hire them to do the appraisal. This can usually happen once you've started a relationship with an appraiser. Some hard money lenders wont ask you for an appraisal because they're comfortable with establishing a value for the property they're going to lend on themselves. When establishing value on a given property the most common method used is the comparable approach. There are other methods, but the comparable approach is used most often when trying to find a value, especially when trying to find value for a single family residence. The comparable approach is simply to find like properties in the same local area and see how much they have recently sold for. Like properties will have approximately the same square footage, the same ammenities, the same type neighborhoods, and the same amount of bedrooms and bathrooms as the one you're trying to establish value for. If you find like properties in a given area that have all sold for between $180,000 and $200,000, recently, meaning in the past few months, not a year ago, then the one you're trying to compare or comp must be worth somewhere in that range as well. If it's a beauty then maybe it will be on the higher end of the scale and if it's beat then maybe it's on the lower end of the scale. If it's really beat then maybe it's worth well below that scale.

Although there are many loans and lenders out there, there may be one lender that many people tend to look beyond and that's the seller of the property you're trying to buy. That's right, the seller of the property you're trying to buy might just be the one to lend you the money to buy that property in the form of what we call a carry back. The carry back loan is the cheapest loan to get because there is no origination fee, there is no loan processing fee, there is no document preparation fee, there's no appraisal needed and no points to be charged to you. Not every seller is a candidate for a carry back loan. They may not be in a position to carry the loan back at all. It can't hurt to ask and you'll never know if they'll carry if you don't ask. When asking for a seller to carry a loan back you're asking them to carry the financing for you for a certain amount of time. Maybe that house is so beat that it wont qualify for regular financing. In this instance you can ask the seller to carry that loan for a short amount of time so you can fix the house up and get it sold or get a new loan on it, for a profit of course. It's easy to ask the seller to carry just by checking the seller financing box on the purchase contract. You might want to offer a down payment on the property in the amount of what it's going to take to close the deal. This way the seller wont have to come out of his pocket with any money to close the deal. That's real nice of you.

If you're trying to buy a piece of property for say $200,000 and the seller owes $180,000, they're not in the position to carry that loan back. However they might be willing to carry an all inclusive note and deed of trust. This way of buying a property is not often heard of and here's how it works. You offer to purchase this property with a small down payment and have the seller carry back an all inclusive note. This note is exactly what it says, it includes their $180,000 loan they presently have on the property. Say they're paying 6% on that $180,000 mortgage and you offer them 7%, then they stand to make a little extra money monthly while they're carrying that note for you. If they're willing to do this, when you close the deal the grant deed goes into your name and you now control that property, however the existing mortgage of $180,000 does not get paid off, it stays in their name and they continue to make the payment. You're making the payment to them and they're making the payment to the bank. This type of transaction works well for a short term. It is not long term financing. Two things to remember when doing this type of transaction is to have your name added onto the insurance policy so you don't have to go get a new policy. You don't want to alert the existing lender of any change of ownership. The second thing to keep in mind is that the existing lender can call the whole loan due and payable if they're alerted to the change of ownership. They shouldn't be alerted because the person who got the loan is still making the payments and they're still on the insurance. There is on most notes an alienation clause though that says if the person who got the loan alienates the deed, the loan is all due and payable. That's why I say that this type of transaction is best used for a short term solution. But what a short term solution it is. You don't have to qualify for the loan, there are no loan charges or appraisal fee and you can close this deal as quick as the title company can draw up the paperwork.

Loans come in all different shapes and sizes and here's where your good credit comes in. The better your credit is, the better loan you'll be able to qualify for, thereby getting the best interest rate and keeping the payment on that loan the lowest it can be. Just as grades are in school, loans are rated as to their quality. "A" paper is considered to be the best loan you can get, then you go right down the line with b, c, and d paper, or loans. Hard money comes after that because it's usually more expensive but sometimes the most necessary. Obviously you want to qualify for the A paper with the best pricing possible. To do this your credit must be good and you have to shop the best lender. The best lender is a direct lender. A direct lender will charge the least to get the loan you're after. Examples of direct lenders are such as Washington Mutual or Countrywide but there are many others. It is possible to go to a broker who has the option of getting your loan with a direct lender for the same pricing as going directly to the direct lender. They just get paid from the direct lender for bringing the loan to them, but be careful because the broker can add some additional fees to that loan that would normally not be charged by the direct lender if you go to them yourself. Shop a loan as you would shop anything. When you're involved in an important deal or any deal for that matter you might want to consider applying for more than one loan for the same deal and then accepting the one that produces first or the one that comes to the table first with the best pricing. You're better off telling one of them sorry I'm not getting the loan because I've got a different deal than having them tell you sorry we can't get the deal done and having to start at scratch again. These loans take a little time to put in place and in real estate time is of the essences. You don't want to lose the deal, so back up financing might not be such a bad idea. You can use the same appraisal for both deals just have the appraiser or the first loan company get you a copy of it so you can get it to the next possible lender.

Hard money may be your best option especially if you're looking to buy fixers. Yes it's more expensive to borrow hard money but many times, especially if the house is beat, it may be your only option. Direct lenders or conventional lenders usually want a clear termite report to lend money on a given property and if the house you're buying is beat up, they might not want to lend on it. They wont have the vision that you do of the house being beautiful once you clean it all up by painting, planting flowers, etc. Hard money lenders charge from 3 to 10 points to borrow the money and 10% to 15% for an interest rate. 1 point is the same as 1% except it is charged up front as a loan fee. If you're borrowing $100,000 and the points being charged is 5, then you're going to get $95,000 once the deal closes, minus any additional closing costs involved with the purchase. If the interest rate on that $100,000 is 12% and the payment is an interest only payment, then your payment will be $1,000. Some of these hard money lenders just might loan you an amount based on the futuristic value of the property. If you're buying for $100,000 and the property will be worth $175,000 after you fix it up based on comps in the area, your hard money lender might loan you 70% of the future value of $175,000 which would be $122,500. After deducting 5 points or $6,125 for loan charges and $1,375 for closing costs such as title and escrow fees and the $100,000 you've agreed to pay the seller, you're left with a cool $15,000. That's $10,000 to put into the property to fix it all up and another $5,000 to make some payments while you own it for a short time. Once you sell that house for say $160,000, because you want to sell it quickly, you've made a tidy little profit for yourself without coming out of your pocket for any money. That's using opm to the fullest extent. Yes the money was expensive but look what it did for you.

Chapter 4

Approaching An Investment

You need to decide what type of investing you're going to do. Certainly owning your own home is an investment worth taking on if it's something you can afford to do. Not only does it serve the purpose of having a house to live in and being in on the appreciation game but it also has two distinct income tax advantages. Any interest you pay on the loan that you have on your home is tax deductible. It helps off set any income you might have coming in from other areas. If you sell that house you live in after living in it for a minimum of two years, you can pocket up to $250,000 for a single person and $500,000 for a married couple, tax free. Now it has to go up in value that much for you to see that kind of a gain but you can't get that kind of a tax advantage on a property you don't live in, it has to be your principle residence. If you're not ready to buy your own house yet then maybe doing a fixer or two is something you can start with. It's a quick way to put a big chunk of cash in your pocket, some of which you can use for a down payment on that first home for you to live in. Just make sure you live in that principle residence for 2 years so you can avoid paying any taxes on the gains.

When looking for a fixer to purchase, look for a diamond in the rough, a house that is run down in what seems to be a decent area. The area doesn't have to be an area in which you would want to live, it only has to be an area in which the numbers make sense to buy, fix, then sell for a profit. If in the area where you live the prices are too high then go outside the area where you live to an area where prices are more affordable or in your price range. If all you have is $10,000 in cash and a line of credit for $5,000, then you're not wanting to look for a house that will require a down payment of $15,000 and remodeling costs of $10,000, that's out of your reach. You want one that will fit your budget. Remember to stay in the bottom of the market or at least below the median price for that area. Drive the area repeatedly and call on all the real estate signs that you see. Also write down the address of all the houses that are beat but sit between two gems. These addresses you'll give to your title company so you can learn the owners name and address so you can write them and express your interest in buying. Some of these owners might live out of town and are not in touch with what's happening in the local market. They might have paid $50,000 for this piece of property a number of years ago and would be glad to sell it to you for $100,000 because that means they double their money. Maybe it has become a headache for them to own it because of poor managment on their part due to them being so far away from the place. If you can see, from all the other places in the area, that if this place was fixed up for a cost of $10,000 that it could be sold for $150,000 then you have an opportunity on your hands and best of all it falls into what I call a win, win situation. The sellers win because they're unloading a house, at a profit, that has become a problem for them and you win because you now have a project that's within your budget that you have room to make some profit on. Always be involved with a win, win situation as to insure your continued success in anything you do. If you're out there screwing people you wont be in business for long. So write the offer to purchase this property and send it off to them for a signature and once you have a signed contract, open an escrow with the title company that supplied you with the owners name and address. Make sure when writing the contract that if the house has tenants there, that you ask the present owner to deliver the house vacant at the close of escrow. This will save you time and money from having to evict them once the deal closes. If they absolutely wont give their tenants notice to move then figure your cost of lost rent and eviction fees into your overall scenario. Now it's time to do some investigation into this property to see just how good of a deal you have on your hands.

Now that you have the house in contract your due diligence can begin. During this period you want to nail down every cost associated with making this property a beauty so you can sell it quickly when that time comes. Spend as much time at this place as possible to just sit there and dream of how it's going to look after you're done with what you're going to do to it. Bring a pad and a pen so you can write these ideas down as well as the cost associated with doing it. You're not over there to build the Taj Mahal, you're over there to spend your money wisely to improve the property as much as possible for as little money as possible. Try to get as much bang for your buck as you can. Try to envision a new buyer coming to see this place for the first time and what might sell them on picking this place as their new home to live in. That's where you want to spend your money. You want all new buyers to be able to get the type of financing that you couldn't so it's affordable for them buy this place. If this place has tenants, it's going to be hard to sit there and dream, so you'll have to do it through a series of inspections. First thing is schedule a termite inspection and when the inspector shows up, you make sure you're there to follow them around so they can show you what they're seeing. If the termite inspection date is out a week, then within a few days schedule a different type of inspection. Even if this inspection is just one of your friends so you two can go over to give the place a good look. Tell whoever might be concerned that your friend is a remodeling inspector and they're there to give you a price on some of the items that need to be fixed. Drive by the house many times at different times during the day and evening to get a feel for what the neighborhood is like. Bring in professionals to give you a price on anything that you're not sure how to do. Go to the local building department to find out how much a permit will cost you to do the work you're planning on. How much will the flowers cost that you're planning on putting in front of the house to catch the perspective buyers eye? How long will it take you to do all of this fixing so you can know how many payments will have to be made before you sell? Do all of this within the time allowed in the contract. You want to have all your numbers in about 10 days. You probably had to put a deposit down once the contract was accepted and you don't want to lose that deposit if you need to back out of the deal. There is a certain amout of time allowed for inspection of the property and the option to walk on the deal, make sure by reading the contract. A good reason you'd be backing out of the deal would be that the property will be needing $10,000 more in repair than you expected. You can walk or you can go back to the seller, either yourself or through the agents and renegotiate the deal. I've done this many times to get a better deal on the property. I've also had people do it to me and I wasn't that excited about it but allowed them to beat me up just so I could close the deal. Toward the end of your inspection period, the sellers think the deal is going along smooth, they're already counting their money, you're their only option, or at least the option they have chosen. You tell them how this is messed up and that is messed up and there's more damage than you expected. You really want to continue through with the deal but you're afraid there's no way you can close it for the amount you've agreed upon. However if they could see fit to drop the price $10,000 you could quickly close the deal and they'd be out. Yes out , out $10,000 and you've got an even better deal on your hands than you thought you had. Now if they're providing the financing for you, be careful how you approach them on this price reduction. Remember they're saving you 5 points and a big interest rate by carrying the loan. You have to weigh the savings. I can tell you this though, the best deal you'll ever get is the one you're willing to walk away from. Don't become emotionally attached to any of these investments, it will cost you dearly.

Now that you have all of your numbers in, it's time to make sure you're going to make a chunk of money on this property. You have the house in contract for $100,000 and the fix it cost is right about $10,000 and you figure it should take you about 2 months to fix and 2 months to sell so you've calculated in $5,000 for holding costs. You've figured your fix it costs high, that's a good thing, and you've picked a target sales price, one that blows all the other competition away as far as value so you know it will sell quick, it's $145,000. You had some closing costs associated with the purchase and you'll have some closing costs with the sale that total $4,000. Now let the numbers tell you the truth. $145,000-$119,000=$26,000. Not too bad for a couple months worth of work. I think you should move foward with the purchase and get this house done as soon as possible. The nice thing is that you'll get all your fix it money back, all your holding money back and all your profit in one lump sum check. It's so much eaiser to hold onto money when it comes in a chunk like that. You got 100% financing on the place so you only owe $100,000. Now when you sell it for $145,000 you'll get back about $41,000. What should you do now? Go out and do it again! Don't go blow that money on a new boat, something that's going to depreciate in value, or any other personal property. Reward yourself by blowing a thousand or two but hold on to that money for dear life. Be good with that money and stuff it away in a bank account and dream of the balance. You've learned a lot by doing this project. You probably learned how to keep the fix it cost on the next one to a minimum. You've probably met some new contacts that can give you a better price on material, financing, real estate comissions, labor, title fees, etc. I hope you bought a binder for that property when you purchased it and I hope by now you see the value in taking that simple test to get your real estate liscense.

Doing fixers is the easiest way to break into the real estate game. It gives you experience with all different parts of the machine. As you're doing fixers you may want to hold on to a few of the properties because there's always a way to make money on them even if you don't sell them. If you have a good product you'll never get stuck on that house. Yes doing fixers can put big chunks of money in your pocket in a short amount of time. I'll say again though, that the way to become rich in real estate is through long term ownership. Think about the money you just put in your pocket on the last transaction. It was $26,000 in profit and all your money back for fixing and holding. Because that house was not your principle residence for a period of at least 2 years you'll be taxed on the profit you made on that deal. If you were to refinance that property and the appraisal came in at $175,000 and the bank was willing to loan you 75% of the appraised amount you'd be borrowing $131,250. Remember that you only owe $100,000 on that piece of property. You've fixed the house up so it now qualifies for some "A" paper financing. Say there's some nominal loan fees and some title fees that total $3,250. You sign the loan documents and get that loan and put $28,000 in your pocket after your present loan is paid off and loan and title fees are deducted. Now you don't pay any taxes on that money because the I.R.S doesn't care how much you refinance the property for while you own it, they only care how much you sell it for when you sell it. You do still own the property and that can be an asset or a liability depending on how it pencils and what you do with it. You still have many options. You can rent it, you can lease it, you can lease option it, you can sell it on a wrap. Once you actually sell it you will be paying taxes on that money you pulled out on the refi. If you sell it down the road you'll be paying taxes on the difference between what you originally paid for the house, less fixing costs, and what you ended up selling it for. Not as many think, the difference between what you owe on it presently and how much you sold it for.

Before you end up renting that house you'd better check those numbers over to make sure you have a positive cash flow on it. A positive cash flow occurs when you have extra money left over to pocket after the rent has been paid and you pay your pitiu.

(rent-pitiu=positive cash flow) You don't want to have a case where you have a negative cash flow which occurs when after the rent has been paid you have to pull money out of your pocket to finish paying your pitiu. (rent-pitiu=negative cash flow) You can handle as many positive cash flow scenarios as they can throw at you, but depending on your income, at some point you can't take on any more negative cash flow situations. Stay away from negative cash flow situations. It's the difference between having an asset on your hands or a liability on your hands. Obviously the positive cash flow situation is an asset and the negative is a liability. You're basicly betting on the real estate market going up or down by holding that property but why not make money while you're waiting. I've seen many people buying properties with negative cash flows, huge negative cash flows, just to own those properties because they thought for sure the market was going up, only to be disappointed and left holding the bag with more negative cash flow than they could handle. In some of those instances they ended up losing those same properties back to the bank and it destroyed their credit and finances. Don't mess with negative cash flow properties unless you have a regimented plan that will keep you going through thick and thin. I'll discuss one such plan later, that I think just might work for low negative cash flow properties. One of the most important keys to holding on to rental property is the quality of tenant you put in there. Your tenants can make you or break you. Don't forget to get a good size security deposit when renting one of your places.

When you lease out a property it's pretty much the same as renting except you've signed a contract with a tenant for a longer period of time instead of on a month to month basis. Again make sure the numbers work so you're not sitting on a negative cash flow. You might get a better quality of tenant because they have some commitment to the property other than just on a monthly basis. Then again if they're bad tenants you're stuck with them for the duration of the lease. When you do rent or lease a property don't expect these people to take care of this property as you have or did. In fact if you know you're going to rent this place out when you first buy it, don't go all out in the fixing of the property. Fix it up to rentable quality not sellable quality. If you don't you'll surely be bummed out the next time you drive by the house. Don't take it personally.

To get a good tenant for either a lease or someone on a month to month basis, make sure you do your homework on them. A good thing to look for is how long they've been staying at their last residence. This will tell you if they're longer term tenants or not. Don't forget to call their last landlord to find out how they were when it came to paying the rent and if they took good care of the place. Drop by their present house if possible. Always ask them to fill out a rental application for you. Study their rental application and look for trends in it. Why are they leaving the place they're living in now? Have they ever been evicted from a place due to nonpayment of rent before? Maybe that's why they're leaving the place they live in now and they need someone else to freeload off for a while until you get sick of it and their stories too. If possible do a credit check on them and see what that might tell you. As I said, tenants can make you or break you. There's nothing worse than having a bad tenant who is not paying the rent and beating up the place that you own. I'd rather have a vacant house than that. On the other hand there's nothing better than having a tenant in one of your homes that pays in a timely fashion and really takes care of the place you own and is slowly but surely paying off your mortgage.

You can also delegate this house through a lease with the option to purchase. In doing this you're essentially leasing the property until the person buys the place. You can charge more than you normally would charge on a monthly basis because the people leasing have the option to purchase. You can also charge a good sum of money as a nonrefundable lease option consideration deposit. The people leasing your property do have an option to purchase it, although I don't think I've ever seen anyone follow through and actually exercise the option to purchase. You don't want to make this agreement for anymore than a year. Beyond that it gets risky on both sides of the deal. Remember when you sign that lease option agreement you're locking in on a sales price that makes sense today. In an appreciating real estate market that house might be worth a lot more down the road. 1 year is a reasonable time period for a lease with an option to purchase. It gives the people plenty of time to exercise the option. If they don't exercise the option you can still have them as month to month tenants if they're willing to stay. If not, I'm sure you can find the next person who is willing to lease the property with no problems.

Selling it on a wrap is as I explained, taking an all inclusive note and deed of trust along with some type of down payment from the buyer to facilitate the transaction. That's right it works both ways. You can purchase a property this way and you can sell a property this way. As a buyer you want to put as little down as possible but as a seller you want to get as much as possible for a down payment when you allow someone to purchase your property in this way. The bigger the down payment is the more commitment you have from the buyer. You're also going to have to put the buyer on the present insurance policy you have and keep it in force so don't forget to get some compensation for that. If you have an impound account for taxes or insurance you'll want to cancel that right away because you don't want your impound account to pay for anything that's the buyers responsibility. You should check to see if that is a possibility because some companies wont let you cancel it, especially if the loan is newer. If they wont let you then you need to adjust your numbers accordingly. Again, get a little higher interest rate than your bank is charging so you can make some extra money monthly on the deal. Be careful selling this way if the loan you presently have is an adjustable rate mortgage because the rate can creep up on you and you could end up losing money on a monthly basis until the new owners sell or refinances.

Make sure you put an alienation clause and an assignment of rents on the note you're originating. Again, keep this type of financing to a short term, 1 year or less. These are a few ways to deal with a property that you're holding. The lease with the option to purchase and the wrap are only a stepping stone to getting a better price for your property and you will have to pay the taxes once these transactions are completed. On the lease option you'll pay the taxes when and if they actually follow through with the purchase. With the wrap you'll pay taxes on the amount they gave you for the down payment in that given year and on the rest of your profit once they pay you off.

Chapter 5

Due Diligence

This is going to take some effort on your part. You want to make sure, at this point, that this investment you're ready to take on is going to work for you in every way. You need to make sure that you don't have a lame duck on your hands. At the same time, this section is called due diligence, not analysis paralysis. What I'm saying is, don't analyze the information so much that it brings you to a paralyzed state. Keep your findings organized and in perspective. There will be a lot of information you'll need to digest and a lot of items to be crossed off your list. You've got an accepted offer on this house and you're in, what we call, the lock and hold pattern. This means that you've got the deal locked up, and a couple of weeks to examine this investment before you're totally committed to it. In every real estate contract, make sure the clause is there, you have a couple of weeks to be able to preform any and all inspections on the property. This is your time to shine. Do some dreaming about how this place is going to look when you're finished, but also get down to some solid ground on what is good and what is bad about this deal. Attend every inspection that is done by any professional, and do some inspections on your own. You want to make sure that there are no variables by the time you move past this phase of the transaction. You want to consult with every individual or institution that has anything to do with or affects this property. You also want to double check your numbers as far as resale or rents are concerned. Be conservative with your numbers. What I mean by this is if you're planning on selling the house after you're done fixing it, then keep your target sales price lower than what the rest of the sellers are asking for their houses in that same area. If you're planning on renting it, then figure your target rent a little lower than the going rate for the neighborhood. Also figure any cost of repairs to be a little higher than what you're expecting. By figuring your costs a little high and your profit a little low, you're keeping your numbers conservative. If the deal still makes sense with figuring the numbers conservatively, then you've got a winner on your hands. Then if it costs a little less to fix, and you get a little more when it comes time to sell or rent, you've got a real winner on your hands.

Big ticket items should be your first concern when starting to examine this property you've bought. Does the place have a foundation? Does it have a roof that needs to be replaced? Are there termites or powder post beetles in the wood members? Is the sewer line functional? Is there water, electricity and gas to the property? Has the city or county red tagged or flagged the property in any way and if so what for? Is there any serious amount of water damage around the showers, tubs, toilets or sink areas or windows? Is there a central heat and air system or a wall heater and a window air conditioning unit and are they functional? If what you're buying is two houses on one lot, is the second unit a legal unit? Is there any toxic mold anywhere at the location? Was there ever a drug lab located within the house anywhere? What is the total amount of fix it costs including replacing any of the other items like the carpet, paint, windows, light fixtures, landscaping, water heater, tubs, toilets or electrical? After fixing or replacing all of this will there still be profit left when you sell or rent this property? These are all important question that you need to find the answer to while still in this lock and hold period.

When looking to see if the house has a foundation or not, you need to look around the perimeter near ground level to see if there is concrete underneath the exterior walls of the house. There are two types of foundations. There is a slab foundation in which the whole floor of the whole house is concrete. With a slab foundation there is no area to be able to get underneath the house. You can check to see if it has this type of foundation either by lifting the carpet to see if it is indeed concrete under there and you can also examine the level at which the floor of the house is compared to the level of the ground outside. If there is no room to be able to crawl under the house then it must have a slab foundation. It's either that or the house is sitting on the ground and that's not good. Slab foundations are good because it eliminates the possibility of having to replace any dry rot in the floor due to water leakage. There may be some rot at the bottom of a wall due to water leakage, because that is wood, but no water will destroy your concrete foundation. The other type of foundation it might have is a perimeter foundation with peirs and posts in the middle of the structure to support it. There will be a crawl space underneath the house for inspection purposes and a crawl hole for access. When looking for this type of foundation make sure you peek under the house to see if the whole perimeter has a good thick concrete base under there. You can't tell for certain if it has a good stout foundation from the outside. I've seen many places that have looked liked it had a good perimeter foundation from the outside, only to find that it was a dummy foundation after doing further inspections from the underneath. Some people will do this to get financing on the house by just pouring concrete on the outside edge of the house to make it look like it has a foundation for the appraiser. Don't be fooled by the appearance of this, look under the house to see if the concrete extends all the way under the exterior wall. From under the house you can also check the floor areas for dry rot and the condition of the rest of the wood members, but wait for the termite inspector to go with you. He'll crawl the whole place as part of his inspection process.

You can usually tell if the roof is beat or newer by the appearance of it. In a lot of transactions, the lender, or the buyer, will require what is called a roof certificate. This is a guarentee by a liscensed roofing contractor that the roof is in good condition and will not leak for whatever time they have guarenteed it for. Usually this period is for two to five years. The cost of this inspection and guarentee is between $100 and $300. If at any time, during your guarenteed period, your roof has a problem, the contractor will come out and fix it. If the shingles of the roof are worn and deteriorated and you can notice that it has leaked in the past by seeing water stains on the interior ceiling of the house, then you can bet that a contractor wont certify the house and you'll be needing to replace the roof. There might even be a substantial amount of dry rot underneath the shingles that needs to be replaced. You can see this by going into the attic and looking up at the roof from there.

When you have your termite inspection, be ready to go around the house with the inspector. Some of them don't have a problem with you following them around to explain what the problem is and how it can be addressed. Others want you to wait until they're done with their inspection and then they'll be glad to explain it to you. Either way, you want to hear what they have to say about the house you're wanting to purchase. You don't want to wait and get the finished report by fax or in the mail because these reports can be confusing to read. It's better to hear the information directly from the inspector so you know exactly what they're talking about. I would go around with him if at all possible to see how he determines whether a piece of wood has dry rot or not. What he does is he has a poker with a sharp tip and he jabs it into the wood to see if it's soft or not. Dry rot occurs when a piece of wood is exposed to water for a period of time and it can actually turn a hard piece of wood into mush after a while. If there is any bug infestation he can show you how he can tell this as well. This is all good information for you to know. If you have a minor infestation problem that is isolated to a couple locations you can probably deal with that but you want to make sure that the whole place isn't being chewed up by powder post beetles or termites. Powder post beetles do exactly as their name implies, they turn a piece of wood into powder, and sometimes whole houses.

Make sure the house has all of its utilities on when you're doing your inspections. If they are not on, have them turned on by the present owner. If they refuse to have the utilities turned on then do it yourself. If you go to do it yourself and there is some huge amount needed to be paid to get them on, tell the owner you want an extension on your inspection period until they get the utilities on. You need to make sure all your utilities are there and working before you move through with this transaction. Check the water by turning on every spot where water comes out. The sinks, tubs, showers, outside hose bibs, laundry area and any other place where there's water should be turned on. Where there's supposed to be hot water check it out and see if it's functional. Make sure that the sewer can handle a large volume of water for a long period of time. Turn on all the tubs and showers and sinks at the same time and then proceed to flush the toilet a number of times, over and over again. Leave it all on for about 20 minutes or so and you shouldn't have any problems with water draining to the main sewer. Don't forget to test the laundry area. If everything is backing up on you then you might have a problem with the main sewer line being blocked, or worse yet even crushed. If you have a problem with only one of the lines backing up on you then it's not quite as bad and you will only have to unclog one individual line. Check all the electrical by plugging something into each socket to see if it's functional. Turn on all the switches to see if all the light fixtures work. Look at the electrical panel to see if it's in good shape. Is there circut breakers in the box or is it the old fuse type? The old fuse type electrical panel will certainly need to be changed and you can add $2,000 to your list for a qualified electrician to come in and take care of that for you. Check your gas by turning on your water heater, your central heat or wall heater and maybe even your stove if that is a gas appliance. Hopefully all that is functional for you and you can move on to the next series of inspections.

To make sure there is no problems with the city on this place, go to the local building department and inquire about it. Ask them if there is any discrepancy or problem with this property you're poised to purchase. If the property you're buying has two houses on it then ask them if it's a legal two units. Usually if the second house has its own utilities like gas, electric, water and sewer, then it is indeed a legal second unit but make sure. While you're there ask them how much a permit would cost for you to do the work you're intending on. Usually it's based on the cost of the amount of repairs you're planning on doing. When giving them an amount make sure you keep it low so your permit wont cost so much. You can also find out about any possible drug lab from the city authorities. If not the building department then go to the police department to ask if there has been any trouble at the property. The planning department might be of some help to you as well when investigating possibilities for this property.

Now that you have checked all the big ticket items and have a total cost on what it's going to take to fix any of these items, go through the rest of the costs on the rest of the house. Decide what you're going to keep and what you're willing to replace to make this house a saleable or rentable property. If you're planning on renting it then maybe the carpet can be cleaned instead of being replaced. If you're planning on selling it then maybe replacing those kitchen cabinets is not such a bad idea, depends on how beat they are. A fresh coat of paint on the inside is almost mandatory whether you're selling or renting. If you're planning on changing the windows on the house then price out the cost of new windows if you're going to do it yourself, and if not get a few bids from some reasonable contractors. Make sure you have the termite company give you a bid on any of the work they called on their report. Not that you'll have them do it because they are usually expensive, but any prices you can get for free you want to get. The more work you can do yourself, the more money you can save and the more your property is worth, this is called sweat equity. All of the cost associated with wipping this house into shape must be within your budget. It also must be within reason of getting your money back at some point. After you total up all the costs involved with getting this house into a decent shape, add it to your purchase price to see how much you're going to be into it for. Once you know this you can get busy calculating profit.

You really should know by now if you're going to rent or sell this house when you're finished. It can make all the difference when determining how much you're going to do or how far you're willing to go when fixing this house. If you're going to rent it, you want to do the minimum you can and still make it a nice, clean place for someone to live. If you're going to sell it, you might want to do a little more to dress this place up to catch the potential buyers eye. I'm not talking granite counter tops and marble floors, I'm talking the difference between cleaning the carpet or replacing it. You have to use your money wisely while fixing a house so you get as much improvement as possible for as little money as possible. Don't go out and sod the whole front yard, throw some seed out and baby it for a week or so. Don't go out and buy all new kitchen cabinets if a fresh coat of paint on them will suffice. Don't go out and replace the tub if you're doing it because there's a chip or two on it, a tube of porcelain repair will hide the problem. Shop around too, for material and labor, there's always a better price out there somewhere. Instead of hiring a contractor, who might want a premium price to do something, ask someone who works in that trade if they want to make some extra money by doing your job on the weekend or after work. You can afford to pay this person more per hour than they make at their present job to entice them to do it because you're going to be saving a bundle by not having to pay the contractors price. Look in the local newspaper or on the internet for savings on material. Be careful to buy only what you need. You don't want to buy something just becase it's a good deal in hopes that you might incorporate it into your remodel and then have it sit somewhere for eternity.

So you've added up all the costs associated with fixing this house and it came to a total of $17,0000. You've already figured it will take you about two months to do all of this work and your payment on the house is $1,000. There is about $1,000 in closing costs for you to purchase this property. You have this house in contract to purchase at $120,000. At the end of two months you're going to be into this property for $140,000 and it's going to be a really nice place that you're planning to sell. There are other houses for sale in the same neighborhood that are similar and they're asking around $195,000. With all these hard numbers in front of you I would hope that you see that you have a real good deal on your hands. Buy it and fix it and put it up for sale for $10,000 less than everyone else in the area and you should sell it right away. If you hired a real estate agent to sell it for you then 6% of $185,000 is $11,100 and you probably will have about $2,900 in closing costs. That means your cost of sale will be about $14,000. When you bought the house you got 100% financing on it from a relative that charged you 10% annually to borrow the money. When you sell this house for $185,000 and pay $14,000 to sell it and $120,000 to repay your loan on the place, you're going to stick a cool $51,000 in your pocket, $30,000 of which is profit. You've already figured this out before you've even purchased the place. You figured this out during the lock and hold period of your purchase transaction, during the period in which you could have walked from the deal and suffered a loss of nothing but a little time invested. Had the numbers for the fixing been a total of $39,000, you would have a much thinner margin of profit on the deal. At that time you could have done two things. You could have walked from the deal or you could have gone back to the seller and asked them for a price reduction if you were still willing to do the deal. This is good due diligence because before you even bought the place you saw the whole deal unfold for you. This is exactly why, on every deal you should spend the time researching the project once you have it in the lock and hold pattern.

Chapter 6

Endless Opportunity

It doesn't matter what type of real estate market you're in or at what point in the cycle you're in there's always opportunities to make money in real estate. Real estate has a cycle that is usually about ten years. Prices always trend upward over the long run but prices do have dips as it's trending upward. When prices top out and begin to trend downward you can bet that when the prices go back to trending upward, they will go higher than the last top price. In general property prices usually double every ten years. Sometimes they double even sooner than that. Especially in the lower price range, you might even see prices triple or even quadruple in a short few years. The more property you own during this high appreciation period, the quicker your net worth will climb. Doing fixers is a fine way to put some quick, large chunks of cash in your pocket but you have to do something with that cash to get to the next level. That's why I keep suggesting to hold some of these houses if at all possible. You don't even have to buy fixers that need work, just buy a house that is of rentable quality and rent it. As long as the numbers make sense you can buy anything to hold for longer than a year. Short term is 1 year or less and long term is 1 year and more so long term doesn't necessarily mean forever. Why though, wouldn't you want something that has the following advantages, monthly cash flow, possible chunks of cash through refinances, favorable tax advantages due to deprecation, net worth increases following appreciation, along with many other options in the resale department. When you're sitting on all of that there will be many others who will want your position and that fact will naturally drive up the price for your product. I tend to lean more toward single family residences than any other real estate investments. The reason being is they are a much more liquid product than multi family residences or commercial. Liquid meaning you can turn that real estate product into cold hard cash much easier. Two houses on one lot comes in a close second and certainly helps with the cash flow factor.

The majority of sales in real estate happen in single family residences, people buying a property for themselves to live in. So if you have single family residences, they have the opportunity to sell much quicker than any other real estate investment. Some people will consider buying two houses on one lot for a home of their own to live in and then move a family member in the other house, or rent it to a friend, but not as many as would be looking for one house on one lot. Fewer still are willing to buy a duplex and live in one side and rent the other side out, but some people do just that. Usually properties with more than one spot to live in on them are more designed for an investor to buy for the positive cash flow or appreciation. There are many less investors than there are families looking to buy a house for themselves. When you're looking for investment property, buy something that's appealing to the masses. While buying for cash flow you must always keep your exit strategy in mind, and you still have to be getting a good deal on the property. It seems funny to say but all the money you'll make on a property is made when you purchase it. The better deal you get, the more room there'll be when resale time comes, and the lower your holding costs will be while you own it. Still, as an investor your single best tool to making money in real estate is by owning your own home. The reason is because you can pocket up to $250,000 per person on the home you live in, tax free, at the time of the sale. You have to live in that home for two years and it has to go up in value that much but you don't get that tax benefit for a home you don't live in.

The lower the price on the home you're purchasing, the easier it is to keep it for a rental. There is a price point at which you can make money on any property. You can find that point by doing the numbers. Talk to your finance people and ask them the mortgage payment on a given house for a given price in your area. You can also purchase a small mortgage book that will tell you any mortgage payment on any amount at any interest rate. Once you know that, add that amount to what the taxes and insurance payment is. You can find out what the property taxes are by calling your local tax collector and ask them what the tax rate for property is. The insurance amount can be obtained simply by calling any insurance company and getting a quote for property insurance. Then you'll need to find out if the owner is responsible to pay any of the utilities for the tenant. Some counties do not require the owner to pay any of the utilities and others do require the owner to pay for the water and sewer. I've never seen any county require the owner to pay for electricity or gas but some do make you pay for the garbage pick up. Total your commitment up and you'll have your pitiu. Once you have the pitiu, get familiar with what rental prices are in your area. You can do this by looking in the paper and even going out to look at a few of these properties, as if you're a potential renter. When you have established the cost of properties in your area and figured out what rent is you can make a decision about whether it's an area you can make money in. If all the houses in your area are selling for $500,000 and the going rent in that area is $2,000 to $2,500, you know, by doing the numbers, that it's not going to work. You might have to look for a different area to start your rental business. If the houses are selling for $500,000 and the rents are going for $4,500 to $5,000 then you might have something, the rent might support the pitiu, and then some, thus cashflow. Preferably the numbers in your area are a lot lower than that.

When I was buying properties to fix, then sell for a profit I swore I would never own any rentals. I didn't want to deal with the headache of tenants. My dad always told me to start holding some of these properties but I really liked selling them and cashing out with my profit. I bought and sold properties for ten years. During that time I experienced two real estate market dips. I luckily bought my first house right before a good market upswing. It was a real dump but my dad said it was a good deal so I bought it. I put down $7,000 on a house I purchased for $33,000. Over the course of one and a half years I fixed it up for a nice place for myself to live. When I went back to the bank and asked for a refi they had an appraisal and they said it was worth $75,000. I couldn't believe it, and thought it was directly due to the fix job I had done. I had no concept of appreciation at this time but that certainly had a lot to do with my new found value, I just didn't know it. I borrowed $55,000 and put about $27,000 of that in my pocket after paying off my existing loan and paying for loan and title costs. I was working as a foreman for a paving company at the time and making what I thought was good money at $16.50 per hour. When I saw the money I put in my pocket after the refi, I held on to that money to buy the next fixer because I wanted to put another chunk like that in my pocket. I didn't blow that money on anything. I knew that money would get me my next house to fix. I figured if I could cut the time down it took me to fix my own house and do it in maybe six months instead of one and a half years, I might have a better income on my hands than the present job I had. So while still working at the paving job I bought another fixer and did just that. I fixed it up in a matter of five to six months and sold that house for an $18,000 profit. Then I did another one, still working that job, and the fix time was even quicker. I made even more money on this next house. I decided at this time to start doing this full time and quit my paving job. As I said I did this for ten years and was good with my money the whole time. I certainly had bumped up my income but I was by no means getting rich. It wasn't until the second market drop I experienced that I decided to start buying properties to hold. The only reason

I did this is because I couldn't sell the properties after I was done fixing them. I wasn't making any money. Even when I was doing fixers, I could only do three to four a year and that meant I only got paid three to four times a year. So I figured out a new way to make money in real estate by holding these properties.

By buying properties to hold for rentals instead fixing to resale I started to establish some monthly income. I had figured out the rent-pitiu=cash flow formula. The property I was buying was rentable quality, it wasn't fixer quality. When I bought these houses I could move a tenant in almost immediately, maybe some carpet and paint. I was buying single family residences for $50,000 to $70,000 and two houses on one lot or maybe duplexes for $70,000 to $90,000. The rents on the single family houses were between $550 and $750. If I bought a house for $55,000 and was able to rent it out for $650 I was making around two hundred per month after paying my pitiu. I mostly put down about $10,000 on each one of these properties. I mostly borrowed hard money to purchase these properties, with a refi of some better money usually within six months. If I bought a house for $50,000 and put $10,000 plus closing costs down and borrowed $40,000 from a hard money lender at 10% interest only payments, my mortgage payment would be $333.33. Taxes and insurance was another $100 and the county didn't require me to pay any of the utilities. My total financial commitment to this property was $433.33 and the rent coming in was $650. That's a $216.67 positive cash flow expressed in this equation. 650-433.33=216.67 Take it even further and let's find out what kind of a return I'm getting on my original investment. I put down $10,000 and paid 5 points to borrow the $40,000 which is $2,000. The title fees and other closing costs total $1,000 so my out of pocket expense is $13,000. Take my total monthly cash flow and times it by 12 to find out my yearly income. 216.67x12=2600.04 Take that 2600, your yearly income, and divide it by 13,000, your original cash investment, and you'll see that you're getting a 20% return on your money. This is a great return on your money and this is only the beginning of a great investment.

This same formula can work for houses that are selling for $150,000 as long as the rents in the area can support the pitiu. After you own this investment property for a short while, you can refi it and drop the payment, or even pull some money out, keeping the payment the same. You can use this money to go out and buy additional properties, thus increasing your monthly positive cash flow. You can even buy properties that don't have a positive cash flow if you know it will appraise for a good sum more that you paid for it. You can then borrow on that property and use some of that money to help pay for the negative cash flow on it. Refi's can help by dropping your payment or by allowing you to pull some cash out of the property. Make sure when you do refi the property that the new loan you get is amortized, and not an interest only payment. An amortized loan simply means that you're paying part of the principle balance down as you make the monthly payments. When buying these positive cash flow properties make sure that the only reason you're buying them is for cash flow or refi opportunities. There are four advantages or bounses to owning these properties and they are appreciation, principle reduction, depreciation, and interest, taxes, insurance and utilities write offs. The cash flow should be your main reason for buying these properties though, the rest is all a bonus that you shouldn't count on.

The interest write off is the fact that any interest you pay on the loan you have on the property you can use to off set the income you recieve from it. Same is true with any property taxes, insurance and utilities you pay for on behalf of this income property. You have to report all the rent you recieve from it, but by the time you write off all of the expenses, you're only paying taxes on the positive cash flow. You probably wont even have to pay tax on all of that because of a simple thing called depreciation.

Depreciation allows you to take an even bigger cut out of the cash flow and might even end you up, on paper, as if you had a loss on the property even though you made a steady cash flow on it. A house is a depreciating asset. The land it sits on is not but the house is. If you bought that house for $100,000 and the value of the land is $30,000 and the house is $70,000, you can deduct a portion of that $70,000 off of your taxable income every year until it runs out. Say you're depreciating that $70,000 over a 20 year period. That gives you a $3,500 a year tax break. That means you can make a $3,500 a year profit, in terms of positive cash flow on that property and not pay any taxes on it. You do have to recapture any depreciated amount once you sell it down the road but it sure helps off set income while you're trying to build an empire. By recapture, I mean you'll have to pay taxes on any amount you depreciated while you owned it, once you sell that property.

Once you have a good loan on that investment property of yours, one that's amortized over a 30 year period, you'll get another great bonus called principle reduction. It's like money in the bank that keeps getting bigger every month. The amount that gets deposited every month gets bigger too. When you get a new loan that's amortized over any amount of time, be it 10, 15, 20, 30 or even 40 years, each time you make that payment some of the original loan balance, or principle amount, is reduced, or paid off. In the beginning of the loan, that amount you pay down will be small and toward the end of the loan it will be most of the payment. Let's say your first payment on a new loan, amortized over 30 years is $1,000. Well when you make that first payment $970 goes toward interest and $30 goes toward reducing the amount you owe. Maybe the second payment will be $965 toward interest and $35 toward principle reduction. The interest portion of the payment will continue to shrink and the principle payment will continue to grow as the loan payment is paid every month. By the the time the last payment is made your ratio will be more like $30 toward interest and $970 toward principle reduction. If the loan is amortized over a 30 year period that simply means that when 30 years is up the loan will be all paid off. The nice thing about this is you're saving additional money per month and you really don't notice it. You owe less and less as each month goes by yet it's all figured into this pitiu formula. You don't even notice it, yet your debt is less as each month goes by. You can keep track of this by looking at your mortgage statment and it will say how much of your payment is going toward principle and how much toward interest. Try not to pay too much attention to it, it's merely icing on the cake for you, treat it as a secret bank account that has an automatic deposit every month.

Another thing that is very similar to principle reduction yet works in the opposite direction is appreciation. Hopefully, while you have these rentals, at some point you'll start to see a serious amount of appreciation. If you hold them long enough you definitely will. It kind of creeps up on you and the next thing you know someone sells a house right down the street from one of yours for a much higher price than you bought yours for. Then they're all selling for that, and higher. You can count appreciation on your net worth statement. When you figure a value, conservatively, for that asset, you'll see that asset increase in value and therefore your net worth will increase. If you have more than one rental in that appreciating area your net worth will go up accordingly. Appreciation is a wonderful thing and this too should be treated as icing on the cake, a secret bank account that has an automatic deposit every month.

Just think, you've got a fine rental collection going on, a business if you will, with a simple formula, rent-pitiu=positive cash flow. The profit you're making on these rentals is off set by the depreciation you're recieving from those houses and therefore deferring any income taxes you would normally have to pay. So essentially your income is tax free. Then you've got the icing on the cake coming from principle reduction and appreciation. It's a perfect scenario. Remember not to get away from why you're buying these houses in the first place, and that is to increase your monthly income by buying properties with a monthly positive cash flow. That's the glue that holds the business together. Don't ever buy a bunch of properties just because you think they're going to appreciate. Buy them for the positive cash flow. Then if they do appreciate think of it as a bonus.

Many times I've had one of my tenants call me and tell me that there is a water leak somewhere and it needed to be addressed. That is a good thing because I've told them I'd rather be called for a water leak right away, than be called six month down the road for a simple pipe repair and $2,000 worth of water damage as a result of that pipe leaking for six months. Not to mention the possibility of some mold being able to set in. But yes I've been called for water leaks and many other things that I haven't been happy about at first. Then after I hang up the phone and begin to figure out how I'm going to address the problem, a slight smile comes to my face because I remember how much that property has appreciated during the time these tenants have been living there and making my mortgage payment. I also realize how much principle reduction I've recieved during the past few years, again, all the while they were making the mortgage payment for me and taking care of the house I owned. So I'm not too upset when I make that phone call to have the plumber go by and fix the problem. If you're not to keen on dealing with this at all, you can always have a property management company take care of your properties for you. They'll charge anywhere from $50 to 7% of the gross rent to take care of all of your management needs, from maintance to renting the place out if it goes vacant. They'll even send in the mortgage payment for you, out of the rent, and pay any other bills that might be associated with the property. As far as the positive cash flow is concerned, they'll send you a check every month after all the bills have been paid. When doing this rental business, it is a good idea to have a few months of payments put aside in case of emergency. You never know when you might get a bad tenant who stops paying the rent and you have to evict them. In this case you'll be the one to come up with the monthly commitment for the property and be the one to foot the eviction bill. You could also end up having a maintance issue that could set you back for a good sum of money and you want to address that right away so you don't lose a good tenant.

Chapter 7

Five Star Tenants

To get the best possible tenants for your house, you have to do some screening and some negotiating. Remember tenants can make you or break you. It's all a roll of the dice but you can minimize your risk of getting bad tenants by doing some checking and investigating. After you know the going rate for a rental in your area by comping it, you need to stir up some interest in your specific property by some form of advertising.

When advertising your rental, start with the least expensive method possible. The most inexpensive way to stir up some interest is by word of mouth and by putting a for rent sign in the front yard with your phone number on it. You'll be getting phone calls in no time at all. Hopefully you can sew up a good tenant with this for rent sign and by telling everyone you know that you have a place for rent. If you're not getting any response with the sign you put up and your word of mouth isn't working, try telling all of the people in the local stores about your rental. They will spread the word as other people come into the store. If there's a bulletin board in the store, put up a notice about your house being for rent. The next alternative is to put an ad in the newspaper. These ads can be expensive to run so keep them short and sweet. If you don't have any takers by now you must be asking too much for the rent or deposit. It's illegal to charge a last months rent although many people do it still. You can charge a security deposit and also a cleaning deposit, either one of these can double as the last months rent. Keep your up front costs reasonable.

No amount of money is enough to charge for a security deposit considering you're letting these people use something that's worth probably more than $100,000. That being said, you have to charge a reasonable rate if you ever want to get the place rented. You have to trust someone and that's why the screening process is so important. You'll get a first impression, but that may not be the full truth of these people. They'll tell you anything to get into the place. They'll put on a great front. Don't lock into anyone until you've done some checking on them.

First thing you do when you've got a live one is ask them to fill out an application. If they're capable of filling it out correctly and honestly then they have scored a first point with you. Though this is a serious matter for you, try to have a sense of humor about this whole process. You will hear many stories that are quite laughable. You'll hear many stories that are full of bull. Don't take any of these stories personally, it will tear you up inside if you do, just try to get a good laugh out of all of it. Weed out the rest and work with the best you've got. Once you have their application, tell them you'll review it and get back to them as soon as possible. You might want to put a few applications in the mail box of the house you're trying to rent. This way you don't have to take the time to deliver one every time someone has the urge fill one out. If you have some phone calls of people that want to see the inside of the house, schedule a few of them to view it at the same time. This will save you time. You don't want to be running over to the house four times a day to show it, especially if the house is any distance from where you live. This will also set the tone for competition. Everyone there will think, wow you're going to rent this place quick if there's this many people looking at it, and they'll move right away toward getting your place for them to rent. Check the balance of their bank accounts listed on the application and see if they have enough money to move in. Never take a check for move in money. For the first months rent and whatever deposits you decide to charge, accept only cash or a money order. I once rented a house and accepted a check. Three weeks later I drove by and nobody appeared to be at the house. When I got home I recieved their stop payment check in the mail. I called them and asked what was going on and they said they changed their minds. I could only laugh. I was upset yes, I had told many other people that they couldn't rent the house because it was already rented. I already lost three weeks worth of rent and all my perspective tenants. Now I had to go through the whole process again. Keep the phone numbers handy of all the people who called on your rental, they might come in handy. You might not be able to rent the house for what you're asking in rent and if so you'll want to call all those who inquired about the place and let them know if they haven't found a house yet that you have lowered the amount of rent you're asking and would they be interested.

Going through their application should only take you 15 minutes. Verify that all the information they gave you is true. Make a few phone calls to check on their references. Call their previous landlord. Call their bank to see if they wrote you a check for a certain amount, would it clear. You can call their personal reference but I don't put much value on this. Everyone has someone that can say great things about them. If you're going to do a credit check on them you'll have to get them to sign a form saying it's ok for you to do so. It can't hurt to do a credit check on someone although, unless you know someone who can do it for free, it will cost you to do one. If you're not going to do one at least ask them how their credit is. Also ask them if they've ever had an eviction on their record. Call their employer to verify their employment. When checking on their income you want to make sure they can afford the place they're renting from you. Usually you want them to make at least three times the amount you're asking for rent. This will make sure they will be able to afford all the other things that come along with having this rental. Some people will try to get too much house for their money and over stretch themselves financially. It's your job to make sure they don't do that with your house. If you let them, they will, and soon you'll be over there handing out a three day notice to pay or quit. You want some long term tenants if possible. The biggest part of handling this rental will be this part of getting a good tenant for your house. Once you have a good tenant, hopefully it's all down hill from there.

If you have a situation where the most qualified people you have chosen are not quite ready to move in because they have paid their rent through a certain date at the place they are presently renting, then ask them for a deposit to hold your place. Just make sure the deposit you ask for covers the rent you're charging for the period they want you to hold it. Also make sure you tell them that this deposit you're taking from them is nonrefundable. You can do this for anyone who is interested in your place but be aware of the fact that if they back out and walk away from their deposit, you're back to square one when it comes to renting your house out. Yes you had the rent paid with no wear and tear on your house but you now have to go through the whole process again of advertising it, showing it and meeting perspective tenants.

Another potential tenant of yours might be subsidized by a program called section 8. This is a program in which the government pays a portion of a lower income persons rent. The house does have to go through an inspection to make sure it's a safe place to live, but you want your house to be just that anyway. You can talk to the local office of the housing program in your area and let them know you're willing to participate in the program, then they can notify potential tenants. I like this housing program because you're guaranteed a portion of your rent, on time, from the city, and the tenants will surely pay as well because they don't want to take the chance of losing their privilage of being on this program. With this program you do have to sign a one year lease from the moment you start renting the place and from there on it goes to a month to month basis. Also raising the rent takes a little more notification than it does for a tenant not on section 8. The same is true for the termination of the rental period. Talk to the local office for all the details on the program and if it's something you're interested in after you weigh your advantages and disadvantages then sign up for it and when tenants call and ask if you're participating in the section 8 program you can tell them yes.

You need to decide if you're going to allow pets at your rental. If you are then you certainly need to charge a pet deposit for allowing them. Dogs can tear a place up in no time at all and leave the place with a smell that soon wont disappear. They can turn a once beautiful backyard into a mud pit that needs a whole lot of work. Cats can also make the place you own smell real bad and leave scratch marks everywhere. Replacing the carpet and pad will be a must before you get your next tenant if the cat is using it for its personal bathroom. Many people will tell you that they don't have pets at all and then a month or two later when you come by for something you happen to notice that they do have a pet. This is grounds for you to be able to break a lease or cancel their month to month tenancy unless they get rid of the pet. They probably told you they didn't have pets to avoid paying the pet deposit. Again, don't take it personally and act in a business like fashion and proceed with your options. Whether you allow pets or not is your decision but keep in mind the consequences.

Once you have selected your tenant and they're ready to move in and exchange their rent and deposits, in cash or money order, for the keys to the place, you want to make sure you have all the proper paper work ready for them to sign. Have it all filled out prior to meeting them so you don't have to struggle and take the time to fill it out while you're meeting with them. Keep this meeting short and sweet. You're going to need all these items, a rental agreement, a smoke detector agreement, a condition and inventory statement and if the house was built prior to 1978 then you will need a lead based paint disclosure and a lead based phamplet. All of these forms you can get at your local board of realtors office. You need only buy these forms one time and you can then copy them to use for future needs. One of the greatest books on this whole subject matter is the book simply called landlording written by Leigh Robinson. This book also comes with a number of forms in the back to assist you with all your needs. The rental aggreement you use, there are many out there, should fit your needs directly. I prefer a one page agreement so it's easier to file and easier to fax to someone if they need to see it. When having the tenants sign the smoke detector agreement, make sure you take them around to each of the smoke detectors you have installed and check their operation. There should be one in each bedroom and one in the hallways leading to a bedroom. Your agreement should state that you have checked the operation of each detector in the presence of the tenant and that the detectors were operational. It should further state that if the battery goes bad in the detector, that it's the tenants responsibility to replace it. If the smoke detector goes bad then they need to let you know so you can replace it. Smoke detectors are very important, don't forget them. I would also supply the tenant with a fire extinguisher that is mounted in a convenient yet discreet location. The condition and inventory statement is there for both of you to put in writing what the condition of the property is and also to list any items that might come with the place such as a stove or an air conditioning unit or a fire extinguisher etc. This statement will come in handy when your tenants go to move out so make sure you note everything on it, good or bad. That way there is no dispute about what is the tenants responsibility to pay for when it's time for them to vacate. If this rental was built before 1978 you must supply them with a lead based paint disclosure and phamplet letting them know if you're aware of any lead based paint that might be on the property or not. If you're not aware of any then check the appropiate box and hand it to them to sign. If you are aware of some then let them know and check the box that says there is. Don't try to hide any facts about the property. Full disclosure is the best policy.

After this bliss period of landlord, tenant relationship is over and the tenants are on their way out, you have to finish the relationship in a respectable manner. Once all their personal items are gone from the property, do a walk through and note all the items that you are going to charge from their security deposit. Once you have a full and complete list, along with prices you're going to charge their deposit for fixing them, give a copy to them and give them a chance to fix any items on the list so they can save some money. If they elect to do some of the items then it's better for you because you don't have to deal with it. If they don't elect to do any of the items, then at least you gave them the chance to and thus seeming quite fair. By law you have up to two weeks to return their deposit. Even if they have no money coming back you have to give them a full accounting of what the money went to fix. Charge reasonable prices for the items that need to be fixed and don't forget to put a price on your time. Hiring all the work out would be better because then you have full reciepts for all monies spent and there's no dispute about what you paid yourself. Hopefully both of you will part ways with no hard feelings toward eachother.

If you do have a bad tenant who has refused to pay the rent then you must give them a three day notice as soon as possible. There is a grace period to be able pay the rent but you can hand out a three day notice even before that grace period is up. The grace period is usually determined by you when you fill out that section on the rental agreement, usually four or five days is appropriate. I would suggest having a local eviction attorney handle the process for you, at least the first time, so that no mistakes are made in the eviction procedure. The attorney has a set fee for the eviction if it all goes as planned. Not all evictions go as planned and it could get messy so I would suggest another method of getting your problem tenants out. The attorney fees will cost you 5 or 6 hundred dollars and the process will take about 3 to 4 weeks. That's 3 to 4 weeks of lost rent for you and if you're charging $1000 for rent, that's $750 to $1000. What I'm suggesting to you is offer this problem tenant 5 or 6 hundred dollars if they move out right away with no problems. You're saving money even by giving them this cash and you just might be saving some serious damage to your rental unit as well. This will save you even more money by not having to fix what they destroyed as they became mad because you're evicting them. No, it doesn't seem fair to give these deadbeats money to move out but it's a good business decision on your part because you saved a good amount of money and hard feelings on both sides. Don't negotiate their security deposit into the deal, use the security deposit just as you would as if they moved out by giving you a 30 day notice to move. Also when they do meet you to give you the keys and tell you that they have vacated the premisis, make sure you have them sign a statement saying that they have indeed left and are giving you possesion of the property.

Dealing with tenants can be trying to say the least. It's all worth it though when you think of the benefits you are recieving by owning this property. You can elect to have a property manager take care of all of this for you but nobody will take care of your property like you will. The property managers fee seems small but they do charge additional fees if thcy have to rent your place out. They also charge additional fees if there's any maintenance to be done. If you are going to have a property manager handle all of this for you then don't forget to add their fee to your pitiu, which now becomes pitium.

Letting your tenants know to call you for a water leak immediately is important because it's easy to fix a water leak right away. If a water leak does not get addressed right away it can cause much more damage. As far as a sewer clog, let them know that they will be responsible to call the plumber and pay for it to be fixed. Unless it happens the first couple of nights they are there, they should pay for anything that gets clogged in their toilet. Many tenants take care of their own maintenance if it's something they can handle and it's not too expensive for them. Some of them can handle the job at hand if you're willing to pay the cost of material.

This is great for you because it saves you labor costs. If you have tenants like this then keep a hold of them. You don't want tenants that are calling you to fix every little thing, that can become quite bothersom. Good tenants are valuable and you should acknowledge that when Christmas rolls around once a year by sending them a card, with maybe even a small gift to show your appreciation of their continued tenancy. This builds a relationship and maybe they'll think twice before they decide to move to a new place.

Chapter 8

Shifting markets

It doesn't matter if you're working in a appreciating market or a depreciating market, there's opportunity in both market scenarios. Whether real estate is going up in value or down in value will only have an affect on the strategy you're going to use. Don't use the excuse of the market in your area going down in value to not get started right away. If you're getting a good deal, then you're buying below market value anyway. Remember if you're buying holders, you're buying for the positive cash flow, so if the numbers make sense on a particular property then there is no reason not to buy it. You don't have to buy them all at once, you can spread your purchases out to protect yourself from big drops in the market. If you're buying for the longer term, the market will always come back and surge even higher than the previous highest high. If you're buying fixers to flip, you're not going to be in the market long enough with that particular property for the market to really affect you. Make sure you do the fixing as quick as possible as time is certainly working against you. You are so short term with this type of investment that as long as you buy it right and sell it right, the market fluxuation should be no deterrent for you. There's always money to be made on real estate even if the market is shifting. It is important to know what your specific market is doing so you can adjust your strategy accordingly. Have your finger on the pulse of the market.

Knowing what the market is like in your area is essential to planning your approach toward investing. Don't listen to what you read in the local newspaper except the facts. The media has predicted 15 of the last 2 depressions. If you listen to them you might never get started or be able to construct your strategy. Take the facts out of the media and leave the hype. The best way to get a feel for the market conditions is to talk to people in the business and get your facts straight. Your title company can let you know about statistics that might be affecting your area. They can let you know about the volume of escrows that have been opened in comparison to previous months. They also come in contact with a number real estate professionals, be it lenders, investors, agents or other title companies, and they hear the buzz about the market all day. Full time real estate agents are also good people to let you know about stastics or trends in the market. They see it first hand as they're dealing with buyers and sellers on a day to day basis. They hear the buzz around the office and talk to other agents who are experiencing the same happenings in the market as they are. Talk to other investors who are active in the market and see where they might think the market is heading and if they might have some kind of a timeline as to when they think the market might turn up or down. Although it is fairly simple to say where the market is in a given period, it is much tougher to predict when a market is going to turn, up or down. To get an idea where the market is now talk to these professionals and get a general consensus. Look at the facts about the present market. Sales data like how long it takes the average house to sell once it's on the market can be a good indicator. Are most houses selling for asking price or are they selling for more than, or less than asking price? Are there a lot of price reductions or are there a lot of pending sales? As I said getting a general consensus on where the market is at the present time is not hard. Where it gets hard is when you try to get a general consensus on when the market is going to turn, be it up or down. Many people think they can tell you exactly when it's going to happen but I've found that the more they think they can predict the future, the less they actually know. Look at trends in the market and make your own determination about when you think the market is going to turn.

The real estate market is cyclical in nature. If you look at the longer term history of the real estate market you will see that it has gone up in value a lot over any long period of time. There are properties in London, England that have been pulling positive cash flows for the same family for over 400 years. During this long time run though, there are peaks and valleys which occur. As I said when real estate peaks and starts to go back down in value, historicly it has always returned with even more value than it had before. In general the real estate market has a cycle that runs about every ten years. It doesn't stick to such a rigid cycle though. It can be less or more time for it to return to previous value and then some. Depending on where you are in the country, the market may have an even faster cycle or may have very little appreciation at all. Talk price with everyone who is willing to talk price. Ask them how much they paid for their house and when they bought it. Not everyone is willing to share this information for some reason. However all this information is public record and you can find it at your local county records office. To track a history of prices in your given area is a good thing to do. I have talked to many old timers who said they remember when all the houses in the area were selling for $7,000 and that they wish they would have bought the whole neighborhood. I've heard this same story over and over again. The same thing will happen to our generation. 35 years from now, all of us, when asked, will say that we remember when all the houses were selling for $150,000 and we wish we had bought the whole neighborhood. Well here's your chance to be able to say something different years from now. You'll be able to say I'm so glad I bought all those properties years ago when they were selling for a relatively cheap price compared to todays market. Remember, all that appreciation is just icing on the cake because you were buying for positive cash flow at the time. Finding a way to comfortably hold real property over a period of time and ride a couple of cycles will pay off in the form of financial freedom. You do have to do a little homework so you know where your market is in the cycle. If you're a home owner already, you probably have a good idea where it is just because personal experience has told you so.

The real estate market takes months and years to go up and it takes months and years to go down so you have time to formulate and adjust your strategy. Nothing happens overnight in real estate, although when you look back on it, it seems as if it did happen overnight. Depending on which market you're operating in, an up market or a down market, that will dictate what you can actually do from an investment perspective. There are many options and strategies within the market that you're dealing with at the present time. The fact that it takes a while for markets to shift is a good thing because it gives you the time you need to make a good decision about your approach. For me, the middle of a market cycle is the best time to operate. There is less guess work involved. There is more play in the decision making process. You don't have to be so accurate with the numbers and there are many properties to pick from. Also there is a lot of volatility in the market in the sense that nobody is really sure what the market is doing. This offers up a lot of opportunity because you'll find a wide range of prices on the same type of product. If it's an appreciating market, and prices are heading upward, you can still get in and have the numbers make sense. House prices are reasonable enough that when you get a decent buy, whether it be for holding or flipping, the numbers make good enough sense and you know they're only going to get better before the market starts to drop off. If you're working in the middle of a depreciating market, and prices are heading downward, there are a lot of panic sales out there. You can get a great buy in this type of environment. Some people are stuck to yesterdays prices and they think their property is still worth much more than it really is in todays market. Those people will not be giving you a deal on their property. Many others will take heed to the market at hand and figure they better sell and save at least a little of their equity while they still have a chance. It's this panic selling time that creates a good buying environment. Buy when there's blood in the streets. Other opportunities will present themselves as well when you look closely.

Some home owners may have bought at the top of the market and now the house that they live in has gone so far down in value that they just don't see the sense in making the payment anymore. They might buy a house down the street for considerably less and save hundreds on their payment and just stop making the payments on the house they're leaving. They know they can't sell it for even what they owe on it so they just walk away. When this starts happening a lot it creates a lot of foreclosures. The banks and mortgage companies lose a lot of money in a depreciating market and that means opportunity for you. The banks have to foreclose if the payments are not being made so they can repossess the property and then sell it to get, at least, some of their money back. The banks are not in the housing business, they're in the lending business and they don't want the property they had to take over to save their investment. They know the property will return in value at some point but that's not their business. Their business is making loans on properties. They have to sell it as quick as possible to regain some of their money. They will be putting this property up for sale for considerably less than they made the loan for. They'll try to sell it for whatever the market will yeild at the time. The problem for them is, that in this market environment many people are trying to sell their houses and the law of supply and demand comes into play. Many houses for sale and not quite the demand for them will bring the price down even further. This market environment is wonderful for a buyer because you can beat the sellers up on the price much easier when the demand for properties is low. This creates buying opportunities in a depreciating market.

Right after the market has peaked is a very tough time to be a real estate investor. Prices are higher than they're supposed to be and who knows how far the prices will drop. The last asking price for any property was apparently too high or it would have sold. The market just runs out of steam because of unrealistic appreciation in recent years. People who were piling into the real estate game because of stellar appreciation in recent years just vanish. Beginning investors who were filled with dreams and hopes all lose their nerve. Real estate will now go down in value until it hits the bottom of the valley and begins to work its way to the top again. Have no doubt, prices will return and go even higher than they were before. There are still good deals out there, you just have to look a little harder. In this tough time I would not look to buy any properties for the longer term. You will get a much better deal on properties you intend to hold as the market scales back from its highs. Unless the numbers make sense and you're getting a great buy, or you're given a property with a positive cash flow, stay away from holders for now. Instead work flippers that are in a low enough price range where if all else fails you can rent the property for what the payment is. When working flippers in this tough time, make sure that your asking price when you're done is well below what others are asking for their properties in the same area. Renting the house is your last case scenario because it will certainly go down in value. If you do end up renting it, make sure you refinance it right away to pull out all of the money you're into it for.

Everybody loves to work and be an investor at the bottom of a real estate market. At the bottom, property has no where to go but up in value. The problem is, even if you're at the bottom, nobody is really sure if you're there or not. You have to just guess about where you think the bottom is and anywhere close is good enough. Anywhere close to the bottom of the market is a great time to do any type of investing you want. There's good times ahead as far as appreciation is concerned and it's really hard to buy something, as long as it's bought right, that's not going to go up in value. When buying properties to hold in this or any market environment you still need to make sure the property pencils. Buy for fundamentals, and that means cash flow, anywhere, anytime, anyplace, and from anybody. Using the cash flow formula you can never go wrong. (rent-pitiu=cash flow) When buying a house to fix up and sell again, or flippers, time is now on your side and if it takes you a little longer to fix the place up, the only thing you're losing is the cost to hold down that property. You might even get that back with your adjusted sales price when you actually do go to sell this place. Sales will start to ramp up as the market tends to go up in value. At the bottom of the market is where the least amount of sales are recorded and at the top of the market is where the most amount of sales are recorded. You should work in the complete opposite fashion from this market trend. Buy very few, if any, properties at the peak of the market and buy as many properties as possible near the bottom. This should make sense to you as you are trying to gain as much equity as possible in any investment you get involved in. It's hard to gain equity, right away at least, when you're buying at the top of the market and prices are soon to fall.

Adjust your investing strategies accordingly and know the type of market you're in. Always do your homework before taking on any investment. That homework is certainly to know the atmosphere of the investing environment you're heading into. It's much like studying a certain company and the fundamentals of the stock market before you buy stock in any company. You want to know at what point you're getting in and if the fundamentals of the company you're thinking of buying is strong. You can always take on a partner in any of these investments to lessen the risk to both of you. Use other peoples money if at all possible. This will certainly lessen your risk but it will also cut into your profit if you have a real winner on your hands. You better know if you're investing at the top, bottom or in the middle of a real estate cycle. This is just as important to know as the due diligence you're doing on the property itself. Once you're done with this information gathering you can move foward with confidence that you are investing in the right house at the right time.

Chapter 9

Foreclosures

The foreclosure process starts when a borrower fails to make the second scheduled payment in a row. A lender, when making a loan, uses the property as collateral for their money and the only recourse towards getting their money back is to start the foreclosure process. Once the foreclosure process is initiated it takes a few months to complete so the borrower has plenty of time to come up with the back payments and any other charges associated with the foreclosure process. The lender really just wants their money. They're not interested in repossessing the property, but they have to go through this process to protect their investment. Once someone has missed their second payment the lender files a notice that states their intention to sell the property at public auction to hopefully get their money back. Over the course of the next few months, the lender, or the foreclosure company that they have hired to persue this issue, has to do a number of things, including publishing their intent to sell in the newspaper so that they can legally sell this property at public auction. The borrower must, at some point before the public auction, come up with all the back payments that are owed the lender to stop the auction of this property. If the borrower comes up with the back payments and fees, then the foreclosure process is stopped. If the borrower is not able to come up with the money then the lender will sell this property to the highest bidder. The opening bid will be what is owed the lender plus back payments and foreclosure fees.

At the time of the public auction there are a number of things that can happen. At the last minute the borrower might come up with the money to stop the sale. The borrower might file for bankruptcy at the last minute, that would stop or delay the sale. Just because the borrower files bankruptcy, doesn't mean they're clear of the debt. Mortgage debt doesn't go away that easy, it still must be paid regardless of any bankruptcy filing. Then again the property might open at the starting bid and noboby will bid on it. In this case the posession of the property goes to the lender and then it's up to them to remove any owners or tenants that might be residing on the premisis. They have to remove anybody living there so they can sell it and get their money back. Another thing that can happen is that someone bids on the property, or there may be multiple bidders. Each bidder must have cashiers checks with them so if they're the successful bidder they can pay right there on the spot. These auctions are money on hand transactions only. If the winning bid is for more than the opening bid, then any additional funds will go to pay any other mortgages first and then anything left over will go to the previous owner.

There are many different ways to make moncy on foreclosures. There are many different time slots at which you can approach the purchase of the property. Your timing has to be good in order for the transaction to be successfully completed. You must have the information that will help you to determine the proper time to approach the sellers of the property whether it be the owner or the bank. Following the property from the point when the loan first defaults, right to the point when it goes to sale, will be your job. Knowing when to try and make a deal on it will be built on trial and error and skill. How to get all the information concerning the property will be your choice for there are many different ways to obtain this information.

There are many different publications that give you the information on defaulted loans. You can subscribe to any one of these. There are services on the internet that will give you up to date information on defaulted loans and sales dates and addresses when a certain property will be going up on the chopping block. You can research the properties yourself at the local county recorders office for free. There are certain real estate agents that will tell you exactly when a certain property is going to sale and charge you a certain commission when and if you end up buying that property. However you get the information about these properties doesn't matter, it's what you do with the information when you get it that's important.

When people get into this situation they are a bit in the panic mode as you can imagine. For you to divide these properties up into what's good and what's not is important because you will have so much information once you start to do this, you can get overwhelmed very easily. It will require you to start seeing patterns in the properties so you can put these properties into catagories. When a real estate market starts to go down in value is when you will see the majority of foreclosures. Some of these people bought at the top of the market and they owe more money on the place than it's worth. They probably got 100% financing when they purchased the property and now the value has slid and they've decided to stop making the payments and live there as long as they can until someone, the bank, comes to evict them. These houses that have more debt in them than equity should all be lumped into one catagory. The bank or mortgage company that loaned them the money to buy this house will end up owning this house in the near future. Don't spend any time following these properties until after the sale date. After the bank owns this property it will be offered for sale for considerably less than what the opening bid price was at the foreclosure sale. The only thing you could possibly do before the foreclosure sale is enter into a sales contract with the owner for less than the loan amount and possibly the bank will allow it to be sold for less than the amount owed, this is called a short sale and it happens all the time. Other than that you should put these properties on the back burner and focus on the properties that still have some equity in them. Those are the real ones to be dealt with when you are working foreclosures. Something with some meat on the bone still.

Once you find the properties with equity in them still, you're going to have to formulate a game plan as to how to approach these people. There will be many callers for these people and they'll be scrambling to get themselves out of the pinch they're in. Most of them will be all ears to hear what you can do for them in their time of need. Others will want to pull the covers over their head and not want to talk to anyone. Some will not be sure what to do and be in a constant state of confusion. Some may already have the house for sale but are asking too much for the property and will never end up selling before it goes to sale by the bank. Really, there are many options for these folks at this time, but they have to make some hard choices and do the best they can for themselves at this crucial time. Here's where you come in and help them with their hard choices. You lay it on the table and explain to them exactly what you can do for them before it's too late. Working with these people before it goes to sale is not a hard thing to do and you can help them out of a tight spot and make yourself a nice profit at the same time. Offering them a sum of cash and having them sign over the deed to you is the most simple way to gain control of the property. Yes, you do have to use a title company as in any transaction to insure there is not an excessive amount of debt on the property and that there are no additional liens on it. If there is still a couple of months left until the sale date then you have some time to refinance the property and probably pull some cash out of it. It's hard to believe that someone would walk away from a big chunk of equity in a property but it happens a lot. Many times these people would be happy with a few thousand dollars and a way to not get a foreclosure on their record. If you're uncomfortable with giving them money and taking the house under the gun with a sale date fastly approaching then put a loan in place. If you're going to make a good amount of money on the house, then using hard money to purchse the property will not hurt you. You're going to be buying this house for well below market value and you can flip it or even turn it into a rental if the numbers are right.

If the people are set on staying in the house, you could offer to purchase the property from them for what they owe on it and then lease option the property back to them so they can stay there. This is a great way to gain control of the property and still have someone in the house to make the payment. Let's say they owe $150,000 and you figure the value to be around $250,000. You could buy the house for $150,000 and give them a lease with the option to purchase it back for $185,000 in one year. This will give them time to get their credit back in order so they can qualify for a loan of that amount and it gives you a nice little profit once they exercise their option. If they do not exercise their option, then you have a house that you've bought at $100,000 below the market and could sell for more profit than if they exercised their option. By buying the house before it goes to sale you have eliminated a lot of your competition that would normally follow the property to the sale and try to purchase it there. You are doing these people a service by buying this property and giving them a lease with the option to purchase. They thought they were going to lose the house to foreclosure and now they have another way to go, a second chance if you will. Yes you've built in some profit for yourself but that's to be expected. As far as options go, these people would most likely go with this one because they don't have to move and they have the possibility of remaining in the house well beyond the one year lease to own period. For you, even if the house loses 10% of its value in the next year, you still have $75,000 in eqiuty to deal with. This scenario is a win, win situation for both you and the seller.

Another way to profit from foreclosures is to actually attend the public auction when the property you're looking at goes up for sale. Properties sometimes sell for fifty cents on the dollar at these auctions. When you attend these auctions, or public sales, you must have the money with you to close the deal, so essentially it's an all cash transaction. You must do your homework on these properties to make sure there are no additional leins on the property. You will basicly be acting as your own title company when you purchase these properties because there is no title insurance when you buy these properties at auction. There are services that can do the research for you to make sure there are no outstanding leins on the property. You can also ask your title company to help you assess if there are any leins other than the one that is foreclosing. Just because you are buying a property in which the first is foreclosing doesn't mean there are no additional leins on the property. I.R.S. leins could have been attached to the property and those will not go away as a second mortgage will. Also there may be some property taxes, utilities, or maybe some city code violations with fines on the property that you will be responsible for if you end up owning the property. Do your homework.

If you don't have the cash to attend these sales, you might be able to recruit a partner to help with the financing end of the deal. If you have done your homework and there is an exceptional buy coming to sale, bring in someone who has the money and offer to share in the profits if you end up being the successful bidder on a great deal. You can do this any number of ways. You could put yourself on the title of the property and then have a note and deed of trust drawn in your partners name so that your partners money is safe. Then when you sell the property, you both can split any profit on the deal. You could even have the note include half of the expected profit that your partner is going to make so they feel safe in the transaction. If you're not big on partners, maybe you can talk to a hard money lender who might be willing to financially back you so you can get into some of these investments. Yes their money will be expensive, but you wont be sharing any of the profit with a partner, so you will be making more money in this way and you'll be establishing a relationship with a silent partner.

If you don't go to the sales of these properties, you could always approach the bank, after the sale, if they end up taking the property back. The banks want to sell these properties as quick as they can and will always listen when they have a potential buyer for a property they have taken back through foreclosure. Most banks have what they call an R.E.O. department. This R.E.O. department is in charge of getting rid of any properties that the bank has taken back due to nonpayment. You can get a list of these properties from their department and if anything looks good you can talk to them directly about purchasing them. In many cases they will offer some type of financing on them so you don't have to come up with all the cash to purchase them. Some of these properties will be a great deal and unless you take a look at their list you will never know what is there. Many banks work with a specific agent to represent them when they get these properties back. If you are an agent, you might be able to represent the bank on some of these transactions. You might be able to be their new go to person when they get a new property back from the foreclosure process. Also you will get a first look at what is available and you might be able to purchase some of these properties yourself.

Chapter 10

Note Investing

After you have been investing in real estate for a while, you develop your own approach or angle toward investing. Having enough capital or cash to look for different types of returns on your money, don't forget to think about investing in some notes. You can be a hard money lender yourself. You can also get your real estate liscense and link borrowers and hard money lenders together and make a hefty commission. Loaning money and using a piece of property as collateral is really one of the easiest ways to make money in real estate. It's a hands off approach to make money in real estate as long as you do it correctly. You do need the money to be able to get into this type of investing but the returns are great. When you loan money on a piece of property, you are just like the bank and you don't have to deal with the day to day operations of the property. You do have some due diligence to do in the beginning to establish value of the property you're loaning on and the creditworthyness of the person who is borrowing the money. After that initial work though it should be nothing but kicking back and recieving payments until the whole loan becomes due and payable. You don't care if the renters don't pay the rent or if the toilet doesn't flush or if there's a water leak at the property. All of that is left to the owner to deal with. All you care about is that the payment is made on the money they've borrowed. That's why I call it a hands off approach to investing.

Never make a personal loan with your money. If you're going to lend money out, make sure that loan is tied to a piece of property through an instrument called a deed of trust. This deed of trust that secures your money against a given property is the only way to loan money. Never a personal loan, only a property loan. When you do make this type of loan, you want to make sure that the property you're loaning on does not have too much borrowed on it already. When making this type of loan, always use a title company to facilitate this transaction. By using them, you guarentee that there are no other loans or leins in front of the position you want to be in. Have the borrower pay for all the transaction costs involved in securing your loan to that property. You can have an appraisal done, paid for by the borrower, if you're not comfortable establishing the value of the property yourself. Even if you get an appraisal done, I would recommend going out and establishing the value yourself and double checking the comparables that the appraiser used in their report. Make sure you get a credit report on the person borrowing the money. If you're loaning money out at a rate of more than 10% and, or charging some points up front, then you will need a broker to facilitate this transaction. It's against the law to lend money by yourself for anything more than 10% and no loan fees charged. There is risk involved in note investing and the biggest thing you can do to minimize the risk is to make sure that your loan to value is low. Also, always make sure that the period that you loan the money for is relatively short. This will protect you from too much market fluctuation.

It doesn't matter where you get the money to invest in notes, it may even be borrowed money. As long as you're making a profit on the borrowed money it's alright. Let's say that you have an equity line on your personal residence and you can borrow that money for 8%. Now you have the opportunity to make a loan on a good piece of property and the borrower will pay 12% and 4 points to you for a 1 year loan in which the loan to value is 55%. The amount they want to borrow is $50,000 and their credit is fair but not good enough to get a loan from a reputable lender with a low interest rate. They're using the money to pay off some debt to increase their credit rating and to do some improvements on the the house. After they pay off this debt and keep paying all their bills on time over the next few months they're planning on getting a refinance so they'll have one new low payment. Let's say they end up paying you off through a refi in a matter of six months. When you get paid off, you pay your equity line back so you don't have to continue making payments on it. Let's now figure out your profit for the six month period. You made 75% of 4 points at the time the loan was made and that's $1,500. You also made 4%, the difference between what you borrowed at and what you loaned at, on $50,000 for a six month period and that comes to another $1,000. $2,500 in a six month period is not a bad profit on idle money. You can even refinance one of your rentals so you have the money to do some note investing. There is going to be some costs involved to refi so you'll have to average that cost in when computing your profit on any given deal. If you have a visa and they're offering interest free for six months, it might be a good time to go out and look for a six month note with a low loan to value.

A first deed of trust is always the best position to be in when loaning on a property. When making a loan that is in first position there is a lot less to worry about. When loaning money on a property for a first deed of trust, keep your loan to about 65% of what a conservative value of the property is, less preferably. Make sure there is a fire insurance policy in place in which you are named as the loss payee. At the time of the close of the deal also make sure that all the property tax bills are paid and any outstanding utilities bills are paid. Make sure you check with the city to see if there are any outstanding red tags or violations. Using the title company will insure that there are no other outstanding leins or judgements against the property, if there are then have them paid through the escrow. Pull a credit check on the borrower and see what type of credit they have and if they have ever filed for a bankruptcy. When you have the title company draw the note and deed of trust, be sure to include an alienation and acceleration clause in it. This alienation and acceleration clause is for your protection and what it does is state that if the borrower goes off the deed of the property then you will be able to call the whole loan due and payable at that time. Also include an assignment of rents clause. This clause in the note and deed of trust simply states that if the payments on the loan are not being made, you have the right to be able to collect the rents on the house. You do have to get a court order to actually be able to collect them, but you can't get that order if the clause isn't there. Also include in your note a reasonable late fee if the payments aren't recieved by a certain date. At the time of the close, you should get the original note and any prorated interest to the first of the month. Interest is always paid in the rears, after it has accrued. The deed of trust will go to the county recorders office to be recorded and then be sent to you as an official document. Keep this note and deed of trust in a safe place as this is the paper you've bought. That's why this end of the business is often referred to as buying paper.

When making a loan that is going to be in a second position, do all of the things you would do if it was in the first position. Make sure the combined loans, including yours, are no more than 65%. You must in addition check the balance of the first mortgage by seeing a recent mortgage statement. The payments must be current on the existing loan and you want to make sure that the existing loan does not have a balloon date coming up soon. If the payments are not current, have them brought current at the time your escrow closes. Use a title company, get the insurance policy, have the property taxes and utilities brought current, have the same clauses put in the note and deed of trust as well as one more when you're doing a second. Have a request for notice clause inserted when doing a second. This clause will make sure that when the payment is not made on the first, that you as the second note holder will be notified. This is important to you as a second note holder for you to protect your position. If the first note holder is allowed to continue through with their foreclosure, you being in second position will be wiped out if nobody bids on the property up to your value. You might have to make the payment on the first to bring them current while you start a foreclosure process of your own.

You can see that even in note investing you have to keep some extra money around to cover unexpected expenses. If you have to start a foreclosure process and see it through to the end, you will need about $3,000 to pay the foreclosure company and you might need money to make a payment or two to the person in the first position. If you are in first position and the property goes through the foreclosure process and nobody is there to buy it up for cash, then you will end up with the property in your name. Hopefully the property is worth more than what you have loaned on it. Your loan should be at about 65% of what the property is worth and therefore someone should show up at the sale with cash and purchase it for the opening bid of what you've loaned plus interest and foreclosure fees. If you end up with the property back in your name then you should be able to sell it for a profit. You might also be able to rent the property out for more than what the payment was supposed to be from the borrower. Look at all these scenarios to project the worst case scenario for yourself and then see if that's something you can handle.

If your note is in second position and the first starts a foreclosure, you want to reinstate the delinquent payments so that you can start your forclosure process first. The reason is that if the first is allowed to proceed, then when the property goes to sale, the opening bid price will start at what is owed on the first and not include your second. This means someone could buy the property for what is owed on the first and you as the second holder will lose all your money. It could also be bid up and any money over the first loan will come to you. When making a second loan, you don't want to get behind too much money that is in the first position. If the first is big and you make a loan behind them and the house goes into foreclosure all the way to sale, you could end up with the house back and then be responsible to make the payment on the first. If the rents don't support the payment, then you have just bought yourself a property with a negative cash flow. You really have to plot out what could happen if everthing goes bad on the deal. That's why when you make a loan, you're best off in first position and having your loan to value as low as it can possibly be.

There are many ways to get involved in note buying. There are plenty of loan brokers that deal with hard money in every area. They even advertise in the newspaper to recruit new borrowers. They place ads in the money to lend section of the classified listings. There are also borrowers and brokers who advertise in the money wanted section of the classified listings. They'll tell you that they are offering 12% on various notes and it's up to you to call and find out where the property is and if it's a good deal for you. How they make their money is they charge the borrowers points on the front of the loan and pocket that commission when the deal closes. You can also talk to lenders in your area just by going into their office and asking them whether they deal with hard money at all. If they do, then ask them to let you know the next time they come accross the next deal. If they don't then ask them to refer the next borrower to you when the next borrower comes in that they can't help. You might get a loan out of this referral and then you can take that deal to a broker and negotiate the points with them.

If you have your real estate liscense and it's hung with a local broker, you can advertise yourself in the paper to recruit some borrowers. Having your real estate liscense, while being a note investor can really bump up the return on your investment. When you make a loan, not only will you get the 11-17% return, which is the interest rate on the money you're lending, but you can also pocket your designated split on the points that are charged for loan origination. If you're lending $50,000 and you and your broker are charging 10 points to make that loan and your split is 75% of that, you're going to put an additional $3,750 in your pocket at the time the deal closes. That will really bump up the return on your investment. It turns an 11-17% return into a 20-25% return. Having your real estate liscense when you're loaning hard money, as far as I'm concerned is a must so you can recieve a better return on your investment and it will help you bring in more deals as well. By having your liscense you will have access to all the other agents in your profession and you can express to them how you're doing hard money and they will think of you next time they need hard money to close a deal. There is such a need for hard money in the real estate business that soon you will be putting in an ad in the paper under money wanted so you can recruit other peoples money who want to make that 12% and you'll be pocketing a commission every time they make a loan that you have found.

Note investing has another approach and that is the act of buying existing notes and deeds of trusts at a discount. There are many companies that do this already. When somebody sells a house and carries back a note for a longer term than they really wanted, or they come into a situation where, a short time down the road they have a time of real need for cash right away, they might consider selling that note for less than the note is worth. You have to do the same due diligence as you would do if the note was new but after you find that it's a good note all you have to get is an assignment of the note, that document has to be recorded, and get them the cash, and the deal is concluded. You should use a title company and you'll have to have the insurance policy ammended so that you're going to be the new loss payee on the policy. You can buy firsts or even seconds this way. Firsts are the best but if you're buying seconds you have to make sure you're not getting behind too much mortgage and that the payments are current on the first. I've heard of people getting substancial discounts on some of these existing notes, some of up to 50%.

There is such a thing as third or even a fourth deed of trust but I would avoid getting in too far down the line in any mortgage position. You can however be in one of these positions as long as the equity is there to be in that position. If the house is worth say $200,000, conservatively, and there is a first on it for $50,000 and a second on it for $25,000 and they want to borrow another $25,000, I would think that it's a safe loan to make even though you would be in a third position because the loan to value will still be only at 50%. You must follow the same procedure you would as if you were making a second deed but as far as being in third position, it wouldn't make any difference. The key to loaning money is really to make sure the loan to value is low.

Any money you loan out on a deed of trust should be money that is strictly extra money and not money that is going to be needed right after the loan you make is due. Just because the loan you have made is due in one year doesn't necessarily mean that you'll be getting that money back in a timely fashion. I have found that people who borrow money at 12% and 10 points are not the most responsible people in the world. It's possible you'll get the money back earlier than the one year due date because they took care of business, got their affairs in order and are now getting a new loan that is a better interest rate than the one they got from you. It is possible also that they scrape the bottom for another year, barely getting by, and when it comes time to pay you off, they're looking for another hard money loan. Worse yet, maybe they're contemplating filing for bankruptcy, this could tie you and your money up for a while. This is the worse case scenario and although it sounds ugly, you still will be getting your money and all the interest that has accrued during the period, just not in a timely fashion. So don't set yourself up to have to come up with a balloon payment yourself, based on getting paid from any money you loan out.

Loaning money can be a very safe secure way to increase income as long as it's done correctly. Keeping your loan to value low is the most important thing, but getting a system in which the deal is handled effeciently and doing your due diligence is equally as important. Getting a check list of things to do before actually making the loan might help. Treating people with respect and understanding that because they are going through a tough time financially, doesn't mean they are bad people, is important. You're making them a loan to help them get their affairs in order, or help them make a profit on a fixer and providing a service to the community. Handle this business with the utmost professionalisim and you will recieve the same in return.

Chapter 11

New Construction

Many investors prefer the new construction end of the real estate game. People who do this are more referred to as a developer or a builder than an investor. I'm talking about people who buy individual lots and put a new house on it and then sell for a profit. Not individuals or companies that buy huge parcels of land and split it down into smaller lots and then either sell the lots or build on them and then sell the houses on those lots. Builders who buy these individual lots, build a new house on them and then market it for sale have their own numbers game. They're usually working with some type of construction loan that allows them to purchase the lot and then continue to borrow money, up to a certain point, to complete their construction phase. Once the construction is complete, the builder must either sell the property or get some new financing on it because this construction loan is in most cases, short term financing. People who do this usually have some type of backround in the field because there are many different aspects you have to go through to get to the point where the house is complete. People who do this prefer doing new construction rather than any kind of remodeling. In most cases the builder acts as their own general contractor and just hires out, to subcontractors, any specialty work like electrical, drywall, plumbing, roofing, etc. Some may hire the whole thing out, including the framing, foundation and any other thing that is associated with bringing the project to a completed end. Some builders have this whole process down to a science and have reliable professionals they can count on for every step of the building process.

When first thinking of doing a newly constructed house on a vacant lot you first must find a lot that is reasonably priced. The price you pay for the lot will dictate how much house you can put on it and how much you can adventually sell your finished product for. Builders usually look for a lot that is priced at about 25% of what their asking price will be once they have completed the house. This will leave 50% of the final asking price to construction of the house and 25% left over for profit. If you think about it in that sense, then you should figure that what you buy the lot for should be how much you make in profit. If you have the house already sold it makes it a lot eaiser and there's a lot less risk involved. Make sure that your final asking price is in line with the prices in the neighborhood.

Before making any offers on any vacant lots, make sure you talk with your financial broker or some loan department first. When you buy these vacant lots, you want to have your financing in place so you can structure your offer correctly. Construction loans begin at the purchase of the vacant lot. They will require that you have all your plans in order for you to proceed with the process. This might require that you put some investment into the project before you even own the lot. The construction loan company wants to make sure that you are going to be successful and that the numbers you have given them are right in line with what they're thinking. This will only insure your success on the property you're buying. The more people you have on your side to watch your back and insure your success, the better off you are.

Once you have closed the deal on your new property you have to act quickly in getting all your paper work in to the right department. The local planning department and the local building department will want to see your full set of plans before they issue you a building permit. This process can take weeks and maybe even months to complete. You'll have to get an architect and maybe even an engineer to design the plans for the construction of your building unless you're proficient enough to handle it yourself. Having a professional do this for you can take a few weeks in itself and cost you a few thousand dollars. Once the plans and any additional paper work required is finished you take all that to the proper department for submitting. The proper department will review all of your plans and make sure everything conforms to local building code and this can take a few weeks to a couple of months before they actually issue a permit to start building. Time is of the essence because you're under the gun of this new loan you've put in place and the sooner you get it done, the sooner you can sell and cash out with your profit and move on to the next deal.

During the wait for your building permit you should get bids from subcontractors on all things that you're planning on hiring out. Shop these prices as you would do anything and try and get the best price as possible. Line up your material prices and suppliers so you know exactly what things are going to cost and where exactly you're going to get them when the time comes. You want to have all the costs associated with this project in black and white so you know how much everything is going to cost. Keeping to a budget along the way is very important so you don't have an overrun of costs at the end that wont allow you to finish this whole project.

If you are doing this type of investing in an appreciating market, your finished product will only grow in value before your project is complete. In other words, you might be able to sell this house you're building for even more money than you were expecting. If this is the case and you have plenty of time to go, in this appreciating market, then toward the end of the construction of this house you're building, you might want to make some offers on other lots so you can start the process of your next project while you're finishing the one you're on now. This will allow time to get your plans drawn and submitted on your new project while you're finishing up with the present one. If it takes a couple of months to go through the permitting process then you'll be ready to start building your new project as soon as you're done with the present one.

If you are doing this type of investing in a depreciating market, you want to finish as soon as possible so you can get your finished product marketed and sold before the price goes down at all. Also, you certainly want to wait before you purchase that next lot to build on because the longer you wait, the better deal you're going to get on it. Make sure there is some extra room in your numbers and that your asking price for the finished product is going to be a great deal when you're done so you can sell it quickly. You don't want to get stuck with the house or have to reduce your sales price to the point where you're not making any profit. Doing all this for free is not something you want to be doing.

When doing this type of investing, it's good to be familiar with all aspects of the building process. From looking for the lot and submitting the plans, to putting on the finishing touches of your finished product. If it's something you might be thinking of doing in the future then maybe you can work with someone who is doing this already and therefore get exposed to the whole process. Getting to know the ins and outs of the building business will allow you to save money and time on the overall project. You might be able to do some of the work yourself and cut out some subcontractors from the picture and save some money that way. Some people who do this type of investing end up starting companies that go out and purchase bigger pieces of land and split the land into smaller lots, thereby reducing the overall cost of each individual lot. You can certainly move in this direction but you must be aware what type of market you're in because you don't want to get caught at the top of the market when you're doing a big deal.

There are many city entities that want the vacant lots in their area built out so they can recieve property tax income. When there is a vacant lot, the city and local governments are not recieving any income from that vacant property. Once there is a structure on that vacant lot, there is income from not only property taxes but also water, sewer, garbage, electricity and gas bills. The city wants these vacant lots to be developed and many times they create incentives for the builder to do so. I've seen where the city has preapproved a few sets of plans for certain size lots so that the permitting process only takes a couple of days. This is a huge savings of time. They also have, in many cases, reduced the fees involved in getting the permit. You can find out about any incentives offered by the building department just by going to that department and asking about redevelopment or infill incentives. If indeed they do have any programs available, they'll be glad to tell you about them so they can get those vacant lots built out.

Finding out about city incentives and special loan programs and great deals on material or labor is only a part of your job as a builder/ investor. You'll have to be constantly on the look out for ways to speed up production and cut costs at every corner. Out looking for the best deal on new lots to build on and perfecting the team of people working around you will be time worth spending. Teaming up with someone who has your same goals in mind might be worth a look. Some sort of profit sharing plan with individuals who are responsible enough to see a project through to its end might be very valuable to you.

Chapter 12

A Balanced Portfolio

I've talked to many investment specialists and all of them suggest that all of your assets should be split up into a balanced portfolio. This balanced portfolio, they say, should be one third stocks, one third bonds, and one third real estate. The first question I ask them, if they're to give me any financial advice, is what is their net worth. If their net worth exceeds mine, then I can give a listen. If it doesn't, then I can't see their qualification for giving me financial advice. I've had money in stocks and they have never preformed to my expectation. In fact quite the opposite. I've had bonds before and it seems to me that they barely out pace inflation. Real estate is the only investment for me. Probably because I've become comfortable with it and I feel like I'm more in control of that certain investment. There is no control when it comes to the stock market. Unless you are a professional at studying a companies internal finances and you feel confident about that certain company, you have to trust a broker to make a decision on which stock to get into. This has hurt me financially time after time. Each time I trust some broker to make a decision on what stocks to buy, I end up with a loser. Every time I get into a bond, the money I'm making on it seems like a slow joke, with no punch line. What I would suggest doing is balancing your portfolio within the real estate field.

Balancing your whole net worth in the real estate market really is important. You don't want too much money in one certain investment. If that one investment goes bad on you, you're in trouble. In the beginning when you don't have much money to work with, you'll find it almost necessary to put the majority of your own money into that deal. Try to work with other peoples money as much as possible so you can protect your own money. Try to work with the smallest investment possible so there's little risk involved. Do your homework on the house you're getting ready to buy and look over the worst case scenario to see if that's something you can handle. This will insure your success once you have moved foward with the purchase. As your net worth begins to grow and you've had successful investment after successful investment, don't get a big head and start to move away from your basic rules that have made you successful. Stick with all the principles that allowed you to be successful. Don't gamble your whole net worth on one big deal, especially as it starts to grow. Keep it small and risk only a portion on each individual deal. Stretch out the type of investing you are doing.

It's important to have rental properties as part of a balanced portfolio. Think of your rental properties as the growth portion of your portfolio. Yes you've bought them correctly and at a decent enough price and at a great time in the market so they make you a positive cash flow, but the potential for growth through apprecation is always there. The growth will come when the real estate market starts to take off in an upward fashion. At the same time it is important to have a sufficient amount of money in cash around to bail these rentals out in case of emergency. This reserve cash must be somewhat liquid. You can put it into a bank account with a high return or even buy some short term bonds, one month or less with no risk, but don't lock this reserve money into anything long term. The important thing is to have it around so you can bail out the growth portion of your portfolio if necessary. These rental properties will double as a stock investment and probably out preform any stock that is out there.

Buying some safe, low loan to value, real estate notes is an essential part of any balanced real estate portfolio as well. These first and second deeds of trust will double as any bonds that you might buy from your financial broker. They will also bring in twice the income than any triple A rated bond will. Not only that, there will be no fluctuation of the principle portion that is invested as can happen with any rated bond. Diversification is not as important as the safety of the investment itself. Diversification, once you have a growing amount of money to work with is a must, but do it all within your specialty field. There are ways to protect yourself financially, all within the real estate field. Just as in the rentals, you want to have a certain amount of cash on hand to cover any sort of emergency that might come about with these notes. There is risk in note investing as in anything, but by following the procedures in chapter ten, you will keep those risks to a minimum.

Having cash in the bank is certainly an over rated event. It does give you a feel of a certain amount of security, but the return on any cash in the bank will pale in comparison to any decent real estate investment. That being said, cash in the bank is what we all seem to be chasing. The problem is that once you get it there, you realize that you need to get it out of the bank and into something with a better return. Unfortunately, if you keep money in the bank for any amount of time, you are actually losing money because the rate of inflation is certainly going up quicker than anything you are making on your money in the bank. You do have to keep a certain amount of cash on hand to protect your investments. Beyond that your money should be out working for you in a safe environment, with little to no risk of losing your principle. This is a balancing act that only you can preform. It certainly depends on your level of comfortability as to how much liquidity you want to keep in your portfolio.

Being aware of where your real estate market cycle sits at the present time is essential to determining how your assets are positioned. Certainly your rentals shouldn't be affected in any way whether the market is heading up or heading down, unless you are just now purchasing those rentals. If you are purchasing rentals, as you know now, positive cash flow is your main criteria. However, the speed in which you are purchasing them will be determined by market conditions. If the market is depreciating, you should purchase your rentals at a very cautiously slow pace. If the market is appreciating, and in the beginning of that appreciating cycle, you should buy all your rentals right away before prices get out of control and you're not able to pull a positive cash flow anymore. If you're investing in notes and the market is depreciating, be very conservative about the value you place on the property you're loaning on and keep the loan to value at closer to 60% than 70%. If the market is appreciating, then loaning on property at 70% is quite fine and you don't have to be worried too much about being conservative when it comes to valuation. If you're holding on to a good amount of cash and the market is in the beginning of an appreciating cycle, you might want to get that cash out into the real estate market so it can make some good returns for you. Get it out there in any way you can, now, while it's a safe time to do so for a short two to three year period. Then reel that cash back in, take your profits and run while it's a good time to do so. If you're holding on to a good amount of cash and the market has topped out and you're looking at a period of depreciation, then hold on to that cash. Don't be in any rush to get out there and do anything unless it's super conservative or it's a rental with a super cash flow. Knowing where the market cycle is will help you to decide how property rich or cash rich you should be. By holding on to that cash, you'll be positioning yourself well for when all the foreclosures start to come up and there's some great bank owned deals on the market.

Always keep an eye on what is happening with your present investments by going through your whole portfolio and double checking all the numbers on all your investments. Making sure everything makes sense and all the numbers are adding up. Double check all the returns on your investments to make sure you're still getting the same return on it you started with. Check all your financing and see if it's possible to get into a better loan on any of them with a better interest rate. Do the numbers forward and backwards to see if maybe a pay down of some mortgages is in order or maybe taking some cash out would be a better thing. When borrowing money, it costs money, so when you are borrowing , you want to borrow as much as possible. If you owe $100,000 on a rental property and the interest rate you're paying on that money is around 8% and you have $400,000 in cash in the bank making 4%, you might want to consider paying that mortgage off and therefore increasing the return on your money by 4%. Now you have to check with your C.P.A before you rush to do this because you are able to write off the majority of the payment, the interest portion, on your taxes and that will give you some benefit. Weigh your benefits and disadvantages and make the decision that makes the best sense for you. Play with the numbers constantly to see if different things make sense or not.

Diversification is another word for spreading your risk out or reducing it by putting smaller portions of it in different areas, not putting all your eggs in one basket. There are many different ways to do this the experts will say. Obviously the old catch phrase, cash is king, doesn't ring true if your cash is rotting in the bank at 4% and no appreciation. It's probably the safest place to be but you're certainly paying the price for it to be there. The banks love it because they are making money on your money while you have it there. Most people and financial specialists got it right when they say to have one third of your net worth in real estate, but I think the other two thirds should not be split between stocks and bonds, the other two thirds should be split between notes and cash. That's it, a balanced portfolio with a real estate theme of one third rentals, one third notes and the other third cash that's ready to pounce on the next great flipper so you can have even more cash to throw into this formula.

You have to be comfortable with the way you diversify your assets so you have a balanced portfolio for yourself. If you have all cash in the bank, it's certainly safe but it's not very balanced. There's no growth potential in it. For you to have a considerable amount of cash in the bank, you must have had some comfortable investment strategy or a great savings plan or something you took some type of risk with. Stick with what you're comfortable with and make sure what ever you're doing it doesn't keep you up at night. Comfortability and knowledge of what you're doing is the key with doing any investment. If you've found something that you're good with and knowledgeable about, do it over and over again.

Chapter 13

Asset Protection

After you start compiling a good amount of net worth, you're going to be concerned about how to keep a hold of it. Keep it growing and don't become stagnet with your ways of building your net worth, but take some steps along the way to protect it. It's human nature to look for a place for it all to fall apart but by taking a few precautionary steps, your mind will be much more at ease. Whether starting a new business or reorganizing an existing business, one of the most important decisions you will make, regards the form the business will take or how you will hold title on any of your property. Given the wide variety of business forms, such as corporations or sole proprietorships, it can be difficut to choose between them. The limited liability company, commonly known as an LLC, has become a popular option. You can even hold title to your properties within the LLC.

One of the first and most important advantages of the LLC is the limited liability it provides for its members. Members subject to any lawsuit may have their interest in the LLC attached, but the personal assets of the member will generally remain outside the creditors reach. Also if the LLC is the defendent in a lawsuit, barring special circumstances, the members are not personally liable for the LLC debt. LLC operating agreements often contain limitations on transferring members interests. These usually cause members interests to be less valuable to a creditor, therefore making the LLC a valuable tool for asset management. Holding title of real property with the LLC as the owner will help in many different ways. When the LLC holds title to the real property, the LLC is the landlord in any lease agreement and long term leases can continue uninterrupted, even if the LLC membership changes. In California, when real property is held by the LLC, the state tax will not be withheld at the time of the sale as it would if it was in your personal name. This would allow you to hold on to tax money until it was actually time to pay it. The LLC can also play an important role in a comprehensive estate plan. Often when a member has substantial property but does not wish the property to be split up at the members death, the member can gift fractionalized shares of their membership interest to their beneficiaries. The property will remain intact, while the benefit of the property has been passed on to the next generation. This technique commonly has estate and gift tax benefits as well.

You can have more than one LLC. Some people I know believe that it is best to have each different rental property in its own LLC. This way if a lawsuit occurs on one of the properties, there will be no negative effect on any other part of the business as that certain LLC named in the lawsuit can be the only one to suffer any loss. The LLC does however have to file its own tax return and pay a minimum tax per LLC. This can be expensive but if you think about getting involved in a lawsuit where they can wrap your whole net worth into the picture, it might be a worthy fee. It does cost money to create the LLC and an operating agreement but if you do it yourself the fees can be kept to a minimum.

There are ways to protect your assets through the way you hold title on any given property as well. When taking title to any property there are a variety of ways in which to vest it. You can hold title as a sole owner or as community property, as joint tenancy, as tenancy in common. A corporation can hold title, an LLC can hold title, a partnership can hold title, a revocable trust can hold title, it all depends on what your intensions are. Asset protection should be your main concern when deciding in which form to hold title. For instance, if you have a partner on a property and both of you hold one half interest in that property and you both decide that if one of you dies then the other will recieve the others half, you'll want to hold title as joint tenancy. Joint tenancy is a form of vesting title to property owned by two or more persons, who may not be married, in equal interest, subject to the right of survivorship in the surviving joint tenant or tenants. Title must have been acquired at the same time, by the same conveyance, and the document must exspressly declare the intention to create a joint tenancy estate. When the joint tenant dies, title to the property is automatically conveyed by operation of law to the surviving joint tenant or tenants. Therefore joint tenancy property is not subject to disposition by will. If the partners are not planning on transfering their interest in the property to the other upon death then creating a legal partnership and having that partnership hold title to the property might be more appropriate. Asset protection extends beyond your lifetime if you want your hard earned money to go where you want it to go after you die. Remember, how title is vested has important legal consequences and you might want to consult an attorney to determine the best form of ownership for your asset protection needs.

There are other ways to protect yourself other than taking on a business form such as an LLC or deciding how to hold title. I rely heavily on my insurance umbrella. Talk to your insurance agent and ask them about a way to protect yourself with an umbrella and the proper umbrella to have. These umbrellas extend liability coverage above and beyond the limits of your existing policies. The umbrella you choose should be enough to cover your net worth, and then some. They not only extend coverage to your property, but also cover your vehicles and any toys you may have. Through proper coverage, you can rest easy that if any trouble comes your way, you will be adequatly insured with layers of protection. On your rental policies, you have the option of getting additional insurance that will cover any loss of rent due to any damage to the unit. This extended coverage will pay to you any lost rent from one of your rentals if something happens to the unit and your tenants are not able to live in it for a period of time. Depending on the cost of this extended coverage, it might be well worth it if something happens to the unit because if your tenants have to move out for any period of time, you'll be the one making the payment and that throws any cash flow right out the window for the time they are gone.

A fairly simple way to cover all your asset protection needs beyond your longevity is to create a revocable living trust and put everything in that trust. Within that trust you can state exactly how all your assets are to be divided up and who they should go to. You will appoint a trustee who will be in charge of distributing your assets where you wish them to be. It's simple to put everything in the trust including your bank accounts, real property and anything else you wish to include. This way the trust will own all of your valuable assets and it will already be determined, by you, how those assets are to be divided or who is to be the beneficiaries of the trust. Because this is a revocable trust and not an irrevocable trust, you can make changes to it any time you desire. Creating a revocable trust is fairly inexpensive and can be a valuable asset management tool even in life. You can own an LLC or you can own a trust depending on how you wish to structure your protection. Each time you want to change the trust there will be a charge to do so as these trusts are notarized documents and you will probably need an attorney to attend to these needs. A trust is a must if you want to avoid probate court and save your heirs a lot of pain and grief. If your intention is to pass real property onto one of your heirs, you either have to hold title with them in some fashion or have it passed down through a trust because a probate court will sell any real property that is left in the name of the deceased and it might not be a great time to sell these properties that you've accumulated.

Corporations are certainly a competent way of protecting assets. I'm not sure it is an appropriate way to conduct business as an average real estate investor/ entrepreneur however you might want to look into the amout of protection it offers and see if it's suitable for you. I like the LLC because there is not a whole bunch of routines or hoops to jump through and I think it's the most simple way to provide protection. Corporations do offer tax advantages that the LLC does not offer, but income coming to you personally has the disadvantage of being taxed twice. Now if you're not going to draw money from it personally, it might be the business entity for you. There are a couple different types of corporations, one of which might fit your business plan better than the other. They are more expensive to set up than an LLC and there is a minimum tax associated with it as well. The problem I've found with setting up a corporation is that it needs to be run correctly in order for it to provide the proper asset protection. An LLC on the other hand is created and then there is little to no maintainance for you to recieve the protection it offers. If you are interested in any special business form to provide for some asset protection you should consult with an attorney who specializes in this field and have them give you the pros and cons of each different entity so you can decide for yourself which business form would be most appropriate for your needs.

Always keep liability on your mind as you go through this investing world. When everything goes well and there are no problems and everybody is happy, there is little to no liability. It's when stuff starts to go sideways that you really start thinking about your liability. Reverse this trend and start to think about your worst case scenario liability from the gate. Not in terms of letting it paralyze you, but in terms of allowing you to do things by keeping yourself to a minimum as far as liability is concerned. If you're involved in a joint venture with someone and you want your money to be secure,there are many ways to secure that investment, but do it in a way that holds the least amount of liability for you. For example, let's say you get involved in a joint venture with someone in doing a fixer that you're planning on selling for a profit. Say you've both invested $20,000 and this amount will cover the down payment and the fixing costs that will be needed. Instead of vesting yourself on the title as joint tenants or tenancy in common to secure your investment, exposing yourself to unnecessary liability, just secure your money with a deed of trust. By securing your investment with a deed of trust instead of taking title, you have eliminated any liability that might arise from the property itself, and you can even secure your estimated profit with this note as well. Eliminating as much liability as possible is a good strategy for asset protection. The less liability you expose yourself to, the less of a chance you have of losing any of your net worth. In the beginning you take more chances with liability but as your net worth begins to grow you start to think twice about getting involved with things that carry with them any large amount of liability. Keep your liability to a minimum as your net worth grows but don't let the thought of it stop you from making good business decisions about your future.

Chapter 14

My Story

I have made all my money in real estate and continue to do so. The biggest influence on me becoming a real estate investor was my father who was a real estate agent since 1973. The biggest influence on me to become all I could be was my mother who instilled in me the attitude that I could do anything I put my mind to. I contribute my success to being in the right business at the right time, being frugal with my money, and not settling for the 9 to 5 status. I salute those who subject themselves to risk , criticism and alienation and live life on the margin to become who they really are. It's we entrepreneurs who take the chances that most will not and are willing to experience the agony of defeat or the glory of victory. Financial independence is what we are seeking and it's only us who can say when enough is enough. Although we didn't know it, the minute we become financially secure enough is when the hard work begins because then you have to ask yourself the hardest question, which is what do I want to do with my life? We've worked so hard to get all of our time free that when that time comes it can be overwhelming. It is however, a great problem to have.

I had been told by my dad, since a young age, to buy a house for myself. He was merely planting a seed in my head that I would never forget. At 13 or 15 it seemed like such a big task to complete. When I was younger he took me to real motivational seminars that I paid attention to and learned a great deal from. My mom had told me always to get an education. So when I joined the U.S. Navy at age 19, after trying to make it on my own for a couple of years, I had all those intentions in mind. By the time I got out, I had managed to almost finish a two year college degree and I saved almost ten thousand dollars, most of which was going to be a down payment on my first house. I was proud and anxious to get back to town so I could share with my folks the things I had accomplished. My first order of business was to buy a house and my dad steered me to a house that when I looked at it I fell through the front pourch. He said it was the one and I didn't doubt him a bit. I put down around $7,000 and quickly got to work on making it a nice, safe place to live. I was working in the paving field and spent all of my off time on my new house. Over the course of the next year to one and a half years I worked on the house diligently until it finally became something that I was proud to live in.

Once finished I got a refi and through that refi stuck about $27,000 in my pocket. It was the most money I had seen at one time in my whole life and it was mine. I was excited and got busy looking for the next fixer to do. I did two more before deciding that was what I was going to do for a living. Really, I was just Doug Allen, a guy who bought, fixed and sold houses for a living although you could say I was a real estate investor. I did that, house after house, for about ten years and was making decent money although I wasn't getting rich or financially independent. I suppose it was something I had to go through before I got smart and started to buy properties and hold them for longer that a few months. My dad always told me to start holding some of these properties but I loved flipping them for the quick cash I was making at the time of the sale. I had heard a lot of horror stories about bad tenants and was scared to rent out a property that I had spent time and money to fix. Maybe it was a maturing process, or a trust issue or maybe I just got tired of getting paid three times a year. The market had dipped and it was hard to sell properties so I went into a buying mode.

I finally decided to start holding properties using the cash flow formula to justify doing this. I was excited about the first one I bought to hold and managed to pull a $250 positive cash flow out of it. After buying about six of these types of deals, I had enough income to support myself on a monthly basis. I started to refi some of these properties to get some of my money back out of them and it didn't hurt my cash flow too much. During this period of buying properties I still managed to do a few flippers on houses that I got a great deal on and I was always willing to sell one of my rentals if the price was right. I was buying mostly single family residences and two houses on one lot but there was a time when I owned a couple of 8 plexes. As my inventory started to grow, so did my income because every one of the properties I bought had a positive cash flow. I was managing the properties myself and it about drove my crazy. As I look back I should have put them all with a property management co. and made my life much more simple. I continued to accumulate these rentals to the point when I had 40 doors and about $7,500 a month in cash flow coming in. That was 1999 and at that point I felt I had enough of it all and I sold about 8 doors, liquidated some of them and put the rest of them on property management. I joined a golf club and golfed 5 days a week for the next 3 or so years. I felt as if I was retired and had plenty of money coming in from my rentals so essentially I was financially free. I didn't know it but the properties I owned were getting ready to sky rocket in value and give financial freedom a whole new meaning for me. I became out of touch with the real estate market for a while as I was golfing every day and really didn't care what it was doing. I had income coming in from my rentals and it was all on property management so it was easy to lose touch with what the market was doing, if fact that was what I wanted.

After three years on the golf course I became bored with it. It was apparent I wasn't going to be playing with Tiger Woods anytime soon, and during that time I had sold a few more properties so I had a good amount of cash just sitting in the bank making a wopping 3%. Around that time is when I made my first loan on a property. I loaned out $100,000 on a property and the loan to value was around 60%. I was making 12% on my money and that $1,000 per month that was coming in certainly helped as far as income is concerned. I really got hooked on this lending thing and soon loaned out all the extra cash I had sitting in the bank that was making 3%. Also I saw what these brokers were charging as a loan fee to loan my money out and I wanted a part of that. So I went out and got my real estate liscense and soon was sharing in the loan fee that was being charged the borrower. I started refinancing a lot of my properties as the value had gone up sharply and started taking the money that I was borrowing at around 7% and loaning it out at 12%. I also was getting a portion of the loan fee so it bumped up my overall return to 15-19%. It was the rentals that had gotten me to the point where I was able to lend money out for a good profit but now it seemed like the lending end of the business was much easier money. With lending being much less liaibility, less headache, and a better return on my money, excluding appreciation, I started to slowly sell off my rentals.

Now from 2001 to 2005 the rentals I had went from being worth $100,000 to $300,000 and I had paid on the average of $60,000 for them all. Had I known this was going to happen I would have kept every house I could have possibly kept. I was lucky that I had kept about 20 doors through this period and there was a time during this mass appreciation period when I was making as much as $50,000 per month in appreciation. By owning a number of rentals, my appreciation factor was multiplied by as many rentals that I owned. There was a time when I would tell everybody about my dad and how he owned a number of rentals in San Jose that tripled in value over a 2-3 year period. That to me was amazing. But now I was telling my own story of how I owned a number of rentals that went up in value 5 to 6 times what I originally paid for them in a 4-5 year period. I hope that someday soon you will be able to tell your own story that exceeds that one. I sold a number of rentals in 2005 and more in 2006 and am presently now in

2007 with only 6 doors. Yes they have gone down a little in value since 2005 when we started experiencing a market decline but they will never drop below what I have paid for them. I will probably hold on to these properties for a considerable amount of time and expect them to go higher in value than what they were worth in 2005 when the market comes back the next time.

Since 2005 and the market drop I have been working with individuals who are willing to go out and do the hard work of fixing a property. I have been financing the properties and the fix it costs and holding off on getting any payments until the project is complete, when we split any profit that the project has to offer. As of late we have been buying foreclosures and bank owned properties. Prices in certain areas have come down considerably and are almost at the point were you can justify holding them by pulling a positive cash flow. In the last month of May we got a nice buy on a house that was bank owned and was a property that had been all fixed up recently. My partner is fixing it now and it should require only about $5,000 worth of repairs in a 3 week period. The last owner paid $285,000 for this property before the bank took it back through forclosure when we bought it from the bank for $107,000, what a steal. We expect to sell this property, after it's fixed, for $180,000 and put a nice little profit in our pocket. Of course I am telling my friends that the way to get rich in real estate is through long term ownership. A house like this one we just bought would make sense because I know the numbers and I know you could pull a positive cash flow on a $100,000 house in this area. The market has come full circle again and we're back to doing fixers, soon it will be holders, then some lending before it's time to start working foreclosures again. Like seasons in a yearly cycle these are the days of our lives.

Conclusion

Wealth building and real estate investing is an art form that can be easily mastered using the right tools. Start your wealth building ways and make them ingrained in you. Use your numbers to check the viability of each investment. Real estate is a cyclical business and there's money to be made at every point in the cycle. Use simple formulas that you can double check to make sure your money is safe in everything you do. Whether you are investing in fixers or rentals, notes or foreclosures, there is a number game to insure success in all investments. This book is a beginning insight to the wealth building and real estate investing worlds that we all should be a part of. Use these ideas to go out and make your fortune. Check with professionals along the way for guidance but not for inspiration. You alone will be the inspiration to become financially independent and to fulfill your dreams to the fullest.

About The Author

Doug Allen was born in May of 1962 in Bethesda, Maryland. He was made in Japan by father Donald and mother Sharon. He has two younger sisters by the name Tracey and Natalie. A military brat he has lived in many of our nations states and abroad until settling in San Jose, California in 1973 at the age of 11. After living there with his family for a while, until the age of 15, the family moved to the Sacramento area where he currently resides. He has never been married but has a daughter by the name of Elizabeth who is the light of his life, she is 12. After spending 3 years in the U.S. Navy he came back to the Sacramento area when he bought his first home and soon after that began to invest in real estate for a living. He has been successfully investing in real estate for 22 years now in the Sacramento area and continues to do so presently. He is also very good at explaining various investment approaches and makes himself available to anyone with a need or desire to plan a strategy.

www.ingramcontent.com/pod-product-compliance
Lightning Source LLC
Chambersburg PA
CBHW022015170526
45157CB00003B/1256